ONE DAY AT A TIME
My Journey with Cancer

Desirae Ogden

ONE DAY AT A TIME
My Journey with Cancer

Desirae Ogden

For my husband,
Mark Ogden, the Love of my Life.
Thank you for your love and patience,
and for always making me feel beautiful.

And for my children,
Josh, Emma, Abbie, and Ellie.
You are the greatest blessings in my life.
Love you forever and ever.
xoxo-*Mom*

TABLE OF CONTENTS

ACKNOWLEDGMENTS

To my kind friend (and one of my fabulous editors), Hollie Parry. I will never be able to thank you enough for taking time out of your life to read through, critique, and edit my manuscript. Your friendship means so much to me and I am so grateful to have you in my life. I also need to say thank you to the other friends and family members who endured reading portions of some of my first manuscripts (which were not very good.) Thank you for your constructive criticism and your encouragement to keep polishing and writing.

To the amazingly talented, Arlene Cook. Thank you for taking on the challenge (which was probably not much of a challenge for you) of creating the graphics for my website. Every time I see that banner on my home page, I fall in love with it all over again. I also thank you for taking the time to assist me with the beautiful cover for this book. You added just the right touches to make it perfect. I am forever in your debt.

To my parents; the ones who have been there for me since the very beginning of my existence. I love you both so much. I am so grateful for all the life lessons you have taught me through your words, but more importantly, through your examples. I know that my journey through cancer was not only difficult for me, but for you as well. It is never fun to see your child in pain and anguish. Many thanks to you, Mom, for the times when you "moved in" to help wrangle my kids and support me through the rough patches. Thank you both for your constant love and support. You are my parents forever and I thank my Heavenly Father for blessing me with such amazing parents.

To my second set of parents, my wonderful in-laws. Thank you for loving me as your own. From the moment we met, I have felt only love and acceptance and for that, I am eternally grateful. Thank you for raising the most incredible son. He learned how to love from the two of you and that speaks volumes of what incredible people you are.

To my siblings and siblings-in-law. I love you all so much and I thank you for every text message, phone call, prayer, and positive thought. I thank you for every time you helped me clean my house or brought food to my family. You are some of the greatest people I know and I am thankful for each one of you.

To my ward family and friends. I will never have the right words to express how thankful I am for all of you. I could not have waged this war on cancer without your love and support. I felt every prayer. I cherished every card, gift, and labor of love. Thank you so much for your Christ-like charity, kindness, and love.

To the four most amazing kids in the entire world. Never forget this...YOUR MOMMY LOVES YOU and YOU CAN DO HARD THINGS! You were and continue to be my inspiration. Every battle that I fought was because I wanted to stay here with you, to love you, to raise you, and to watch you grow. My number one prayer is for you to remember that it was our Savior who helped us through this hard time in our lives. He was the one that carried us and He will carry you through all the hard times to come, but you must turn to Him. He will always love you no matter what, and so will I.

To the Love of My Life. Where do I begin? In 2011, we started on this journey that was not part of any of the plans we had made for our lives. You are my rock. I could not have survived this without you. I remember hearing stories from other breast cancer patients about how their spouses or significant others left them when the going got tough. I could not fathom what that felt like because I only felt love and encouragement from you. You never made me feel like I was a

2

~ACKNOWLEDGMENTS~

burden. You never complained to me about the countless hours you had to spend in doctor's offices and waiting rooms. You only made me feel beautiful and loved. It has been a rough road and I am sure that there will be many more rough roads to travel, but with you by my side for eternity, I know that all will be well. I love you.

INTRODUCTION

I have never attempted something like this before--this whole "writing a book" thing. I survived my high school English classes because I had great teachers. I enjoy writing in my journal but am sporadic at best in the consistency of the entries. I love keeping up my blog and have found that it gives me an outlet to express my faith, fears, frustrations, and joy.

Now I want to take that love and write a whole book? One that people, besides my mother, will actually want to read? No, I have never attempted anything like this. I guess it's just one more item to add to the list; the list of things that cancer has brought into my life. But you know what? I can do hard things, like write an entire, amazing, and inspiring book, so stick with me. I promise you will laugh, cry, and leave with more confidence in the fact that YOU CAN ALSO DO HARD THINGS.

When I sat down and started brainstorming how this was all going to go, I thought it would be best to start with some goals. I believe that having goals will bring clarity and focus to this task. My three goals for this book are as follows:

1. To inspire people who are in the trenches of a war with cancer.
2. To inspire mothers.
3. To share my love for and testimony of our Savior, Jesus Christ.

~INTRODUCTION~

So how do I go about writing a book? I am trying to dig down into the deep, dark recesses of my brain and find the information that my 10th grade English teacher, Mrs. J. taught me. I learned a lot about writing while sitting in that English class. She has a passion for writing that is still impressed upon my mind after 20+ years. Now if I can just get the rusty wheels turning in my post-pregnancy and chemo-poisoned brain, I'll be in good shape. Here goes nothing.

PART ONE

One: 8-19-11

August 19, 2011, started out beautifully. I watched with excitement, nervousness, and a little bit of sadness as my oldest child, Josh, got ready for his first day of junior high school. How did he get so big? I remember him toddling around on chubby little legs learning how to walk. Now I had to drop him off at the junior high so he could learn to walk through the seemingly endless supply of hallways and staircases there.

We pulled up to the school and after kissing his mother on the cheek, he jumped out of the car. With confidence and excitement oozing from every ounce of his 7th grade body, he strode off without even so much as a glance back in my direction. I suppose I had no need to be nervous. He was ready for the challenge.

My girls still had a few days before their school would begin. We had plans that day to enjoy the last of our summer freedom. Those plans included a figure skating lesson for Emma, and after looking at our bare cupboards, a trip to Costco as well.

After Emma's lesson, we were piling into the van when my phone started to ring. I was expecting a phone call from the Women's Center at St. Mark's Hospital because I had gone in for a biopsy the day before. I knew that this would be the call to tell me that the tissue from the lump in my right breast had been tested and the results were exactly what we thought they would be; it was just a fibrous mass and nothing else.

"Hello?" I said as I was juggling my phone, my purse, and attempting to buckle Ellie into her car seat.

"Hello? Is this Desirae?" asked a kind, yet businesslike voice.

"Yes, this is she."

"Hi, Desirae. This is Dr. O'Neill. We got the results back from your biopsy and I am very sorry to say that things do not look good. I hate to tell you this over the phone, but there were some cancer cells that showed up. I'm very sorry." (There was silence on my end for what felt like an eternity as my brain tried to process this information.)

"Really. Wow," is what I finally choked out.

Have you ever wondered what you might do or say if you are told you have cancer? I have thought about it on occasion, but it was nothing that I pondered too deeply about. Cancer was something that happened to other people, not to me. I didn't have time for cancer in my busy life. I had groceries to buy, kids to cart around, and a life to live. I simply could not add cancer to my plate, so I got in my car and started driving. Maybe I was hoping that I could drive away from this stunning turn of events.

While I was driving, Dr. O'Neill was still talking away in my ear. I was hearing words like "MRI", "Grade 2 Cancer", "Surgeon", and a million other things. Why didn't I pull over and start writing these things down? Because I was in shock and avoidance mode, that's why.

With Dr. O'Neill still talking in one ear and my girls asking me, "Mom, what's wrong?" in the other, I knew that I needed only one thing--my husband. I needed him to wrap his arms around me and hug me tight. I also needed to hear him say that everything was going to be all right. Suddenly, my driving had a purpose and that was to get to his office as quickly as I could.

Now that I was headed in the right direction, I could concentrate a bit more on the conversation with Dr. O'Neill.

"I will call Dr. Mainwaring to discuss some things with her. I will also arrange for you to come in for an MRI tonight. I will get back to you soon," she said.

I tossed my phone on the passenger seat and tried to keep my wits about me. I did not want to start crying while I was driving. The tears were obedient and stayed in check until I pulled up to Mark's work. That was when the dam broke and I couldn't hold them in any longer. I could sense my girls' nervousness increase when they saw the tears rolling down my cheeks. I told them, "It's okay. Everything is okay. I just need to talk to Daddy for a minute."

I called Mark and told him that I was sitting in the parking lot and that I needed to see him right away. When I saw him through the glass doors of his office building, I flung my car door open and ran to meet him. I tried to form the right words to say while the tears rolled down my cheeks. "They found cancer. They found cancer," I cried out through my tears. I was trying to remember everything that Dr. O'Neill had told me, but it was all a jumbled mess in my brain.

I know that Mark must have felt overwhelmed with the scene before him. He had his sobbing wife clinging to him while shouting the word "cancer" at him. The faces of his three bewildered girls were pressed against the van windows; the looks of fear and confusion clearly present.

I am sure that he was also trying to find the right words to say. With this scene laid out before him, he did exactly what I needed him to do. He hugged me and told me not to worry. He said that we would just take things one at a time and figure it all out. We hugged for a long time. His embrace was rejuvenating. I did not want to let him go because I felt safe in his hug and I knew that as soon as I let him go, I would have to face this new horror head on.

Eventually, we stopped hugging and I was able to gain some composure. I wiped the tears away and told him that I would let him know when I heard back from the doctor. Then I sent him back to work, holding this new information like one would hold a porcupine-- not quite sure of how to handle it. Finally, I got back into the van and the girls and I were off to Costco because I didn't have time to deal with cancer and we needed groceries.

Two: MEET THE OGDENS

Before I continue with my cancer journey, I would like to take a moment to talk about how our family came to be and what our life was like before 8-19-11 because my family played a pivotal role in my journey. Every decision I made regarding cancer was made with them in mind. They were the reason I refused to give up, even when I felt like I couldn't take one more step.

Rewind to the summer of 1997. I had just about given up on any prospect of marriage. I had reached the ripe old age of 19 and knew that I was doomed to live the life of a spinster. Can you say crazy?

I had graduated from high school and spent one semester fumbling around at Dixie College in St. George, Utah. After this short-lived college experience, I decided to move to the huge metropolis of Salt Lake City, Utah, and join the working force for a while. My grandparents were kind enough to let me live with them and I settled into a job as a teller at a credit union.

I had a few friends from work that I would occasionally hang out with, but most of my nights were spent hanging out with my grandparents. It was a pretty exciting life for a 19-year-old spinster. I did go on a few dates and had some *interesting* experiences that left me a bit scarred. These experiences left me wondering if I should just move back home, give up dating altogether, and try the college thing again. That was when I went on a blind date with Mark Ogden that changed my life forever.

This fateful date was the result of a scheme hatched in a quaint little beauty shop. Mark's mother is a hairdresser. She owns a beauty shop and has many ladies who make the weekly pilgrimage to her shop to have their hair done. My Aunt Jeanne is included in that wonderful group of ladies. In that shop, conversation (in other words, gossip) flows as thick as the hairspray that covers their newly backcombed hairdos.

The "conversation" in the shop at that time was focused on how to get Mark to call me. He had recently returned from serving a mission for our church, The Church of Jesus Christ of Latter-Day Saints. After living in Taiwan for two years, he was completely content with camping out on the couch, catching up on all the movies he had missed. He was not interested in calling the "cute girl" that one of his mom's ladies wanted to set him up with.

I, however, was in desperation mode. When my aunt told me about Mark, I had no problem calling this strange guy to see if he would accompany me to a work party. I tried calling him a few times, but couldn't reach him.

"Oh well," I thought. "I guess it's not meant to be." Back to my plans of packing it up and moving back home.

Shortly thereafter, as I was arriving home from work one day, I received a phone call from my Aunt Jeanne.

"You need to call Mark right away! He is waiting for you to call him," she said.

"Umm, okay," I responded. I was thinking to myself, "Why is he not just calling me?" But hey, beggars can't be choosers, right? A date is a date. So, I picked up the phone and gave him a call. He invited me to go on a double date to the movies that night. As in, I had 15 minutes to get ready.

I took a quick assessment of my appearance. Let's see, ball cap on the head to cover my bad hair day? Check. How about some baggy overalls to accentuate all my alluring curves? Check. It was the perfect situation for a blind date. Bring it on.

I hung up the phone and made a mad dash to my room to find another outfit. Unfortunately, the process came to a screeching halt when I realized that what I was wearing was the only clean thing available. Blast! Why didn't I use my day off to throw in a load of laundry? Time for Plan B. Maybe I could make something nice out of this mess on my head that would draw the attention away from my outfit. I ran to the bathroom and used every hair product I owned with no success; still an abomination. A ball cap was the only viable option at this point.

The doorbell rang. I said a quick prayer that my sweet spirit would come shining through and Mark wouldn't notice how sloppy I looked. I opened the door and my first thought was, "Oh man! He's cute too! Why do I have to look like such a slob today of all days?"

We left on our date and an amazing thing happened that night. One would assume that I would have been uncomfortable the whole time because of how I looked and the fact that it was a blind date. However, the exact opposite happened. I found myself feeling completely relaxed. Mark was so easy to talk to. I felt as if I had known him forever.

Two days later we talked on the phone for over an hour and by the end of the phone call, we had dates lined up for the next two Saturdays. Two and a half weeks later, we were engaged. (The time frame varies depending on whom you are talking to, but it's my book, so two and a half weeks it is.)

It was definitely a case of "when you know, you know." I felt at home with Mark and his family. I believe that we lived before we came to this earth as spirit children of a loving father in Heaven. I also believe, rather know, that Mark and I knew each other in that life. We knew that we wanted to be together as husband and wife and when we met each other here, those feelings were present.

Mark is the love of my life and on a beautiful, but freezing cold day in December, we were married in the Salt Lake Temple. We will be together forever.

There is no "until death do us part" in this scenario. We made covenants with each other, and with God, across an altar in a holy temple. This fact alone was a source of comfort even on the darkest days of my journey with cancer.

Life moved along, as it tends to do, and it wasn't long before our little family of two turned into three. I then began the best and most difficult job of my life--being a mommy.

My little Joshua Squashua was born in 1999. When my water broke, I knew that my life would never be the same again. I was scared out of my mind, but was also looking forward to the challenge because being a mom was all I ever really wanted to do.

I loved my life as a new mommy so much. I never imagined how much I could love this squishy little boy of mine or how tired I would be in trying to keep up with him. My days were filled with diapers and laundry, joy, and tears (his AND mine) as I tried to figure this whole mommy business out. It was harder than I ever thought it would be, but so worth it.

I loved hearing his little voice. I loved having his pudgy fingers intertwined with mine. I did not, however, love potty training, sleepless nights, or worrying about a sick baby. Having said that, I have discovered something that I dislike more than potty training: teaching a 15-year-old boy how to drive. Give me the potty training any day.

A few years went by and in 2002 our first little princess was born, my sweet Emma Lemma Ding Dong. Josh was completely smitten with his little sister and stopped referring to himself as Josh. He was now "Emma's big brother."

Everything seemed to be perfect. I had two healthy (and adorable) children. Mark and I were happy in our marriage and we had settled into a great routine. Then, I missed a period. Eight months later, my second princess, Abbie Kadabbie, came into this world.

I like to say that Abbie has been doing exactly what she wants to do since before she was born. She was born just 22 months after Emma, which was not in my original plan of how we would space our kids apart. This would mean I would have two in diapers, which was not fun, but having a beautiful baby to snuggle made up for that.

I really wanted to be done having kids after Abbie. I loved my kiddos fiercely, but I did not enjoy being pregnant. However, I could not shake the feeling that there was someone else waiting to come to our family.

My third princess, Ellie Bellie, was born in 2006. The whole time I was pregnant with her, I knew that it would be the last pregnancy for me. I tried to enjoy every moment of it, even the uncomfortable ones. When we brought Miss Ellie home a few weeks before Christmas, we felt complete.

Let's fast forward to 2011. Life was good. Josh was now old enough to watch the girls while I ran an errand or two. For me, reaching this milestone in my life was just about as close to heaven on earth as I could get. No longer did I have to make a dreaded trip to the store with four little munchkins in tow. I could actually make it through the store without having to break up a disagreement, look for a lost kid in the clothes racks, or put on my smiling "wait until we get home" face.

Mark and I were also doing well at this time in our lives. We were enjoying good health and happiness. We had taken a trip to Hawaii to celebrate our 13th wedding anniversary where we were able to relax and reflect on where our lives had taken us. We both felt an immense surge of gratitude for all the blessings in our lives.

This brings us to the summer of 2011, which had been particularly wonderful. We had redecorated bedrooms, played at parks, gone to movies, and spent lots of lazy afternoons together.

As the summer was winding down, there was "new school year" excitement in the air. The kids were all set with new clothes and school supplies. I was set to have a quiet year at home with only Ellie to keep me company. That's when I received that fateful phone call which sent our cozy little life into a tailspin.

~ONE DAY AT A TIME~

My cute family in July 2011

Three: THE LUMP

Before the phone call I received on that August morning, came "The Lump." It was smallish in size, but the fact that it was there was a glaring sign that something was not quite right.

The first time I felt it was when I was scratching an itch close to my right armpit. I noted that the lump was about the size of a large pea. It was a little tender if I gently squeezed it and I could also roll it around a bit with my fingers. Even though Mark was driving us to our family reunion at the time I made this discovery, I made him reach over so he could feel it.

"Do you remember that being there before?" I asked.

"No," he replied.

"Hmm. I don't remember it being there either. I will have to ask Dr. Mainwaring about it when I see her in a couple of weeks."

When I went to that next scheduled appointment, I almost forgot to talk to her about The Lump. We got caught up in discussing my irregular periods and it must have slipped my mind. But thanks to divine intervention, I remembered The Lump just as my doctor was about to leave the room.

"By the way," I said, "I found this lump a couple of weeks ago. Could you please check it out?"

She looked at it, felt it, and asked me questions about it.

"Is it painful?" she asked.

"Only if I apply a little pressure to it," I replied.

"Does it move if you try to roll it with your fingers?"

"Yes, a little bit," I said.

"Oh good," she replied. "Then it is probably not cancer because typically, a cancer tumor is not painful. Also, you would probably not be able to move it around so much if it was cancer."

We both thought that the lump was maybe a cyst brought on by the hormone treatments that I had been doing. Neither of us were overly concerned that it was cancer.

I left her office with instructions to continue the birth control pills I was on and to watch The Lump for a couple of weeks. If it did not go away, or if it got bigger, I was to go and have an ultrasound. I made my way home and did not have another thought about The Lump.

My busy life consumed me and it wasn't until a couple of weeks later that I remembered The Lump. I was trying to get a handle on the Mount Vesuvius of paperwork on my kitchen counter and I came across the ultrasound order.

I immediately felt for The Lump. Yes, it was still there. Wait a second. Was it bigger? At that moment, I had the distinct impression to stop sorting through papers and call to schedule an ultrasound. Fortunately, they were able to schedule me for that week.

I went in for a breast ultrasound on August 12th. While the nurse was taking me back to change my clothes, she said, "The radiologist would like you to have a mammogram as well since you are over 30 and have found a lump."

"Sure! Why not?" I thought. "Let's go squish my boobs." That surprise turn of events made the anxiety start to creep in a bit. I didn't know what to expect from a mammogram and I had not mentally prepared myself for one either. I was just there to get an ultrasound and be on my merry way.

As I sat by myself in the waiting room, I tried to settle the uneasiness growing in my heart by flipping through some magazines. We couldn't really be talking about cancer here, could we? Finally, it was my turn and I followed the nurse back to the mammography room.

Thankfully, and to my great surprise, the mammogram was easy, although a tad uncomfortable. The only thing that presented a bit of a challenge was the fact that I had breast implants.

In 2009, I had made the decision to have breast augmentation surgery. A lot of thought and prayer went into that major decision and I have never regretted doing it. In fact, I now feel like the implants played a small part in saving my life. Because of the location of the lump, I don't think I would have felt it as soon as I did if the implants had not been there.

The mammography technician was very proficient at her job and positioned me where I needed to be so that she could get a good image. She helped me feel at ease and I went back to not being anxious at all. When the mammogram was over, I was taken to another room to have the ultrasound.

Again, I was impressed with the professionalism and kindness of the technician who took care of me. She took the images she needed and then had the radiologist come in to take more images. Dr. O'Neill, the radiologist, said that the mammogram images looked good. In fact, because of where the lump was located, it did not even show up on the mammogram. (*Here is where I must insert my plug for self-breast exams. They are a good defense in finding a problem. Sometimes mammograms do not pick things up. When it comes right down to it, you know your body. Listen to it and do your monthly self-exams!*)

Dr. O'Neill then went on to say that she still wanted to investigate The Lump further by having me come back in a few days to do a needle biopsy. That way we would know for sure what we were dealing with. That sounded fine to me. Let's do the biopsy and then we would know that it was just a cyst or fibroid and I could get on with my regular life.

On August 18th, I went in for the biopsy. The first step in the biopsy process was to numb the area. That was a necessity because in step number two, they brought out a needle the size of a straw and jabbed it into my breast. As I watched the monitor, I could see the needle plunging into the depths of my breast

19

tissue. It was very strange to see this foreign object going deeper into by breast, but not feel anything at all. Thank you, Lidocaine.

I was so caught up in looking at the image on the screen, that I almost missed it when the radiologist said, "Hmm. That feels different than I expected it to. It is much harder. Not to worry, though. It could still be a fibroid. We'll see what the pathology report says."

A wave of worry rushed at me, but I quickly brushed it off. There was absolutely no way this could be breast cancer. I was only 33 years old and there was no history of breast cancer in my family. I was healthy and I guess I felt a little invincible. Cancer couldn't happen to me.

That was my thought process as I changed out of the hospital gown and into my own clothes. The nurse asked me how I would like to receive the results of the biopsy. The options were, to schedule a time to go into the office the following day or to just receive a phone call.

"Oh, just call me," I said.

I did not want to make a trip back to the hospital to have them say that it was just a fibroid. I thanked the staff, grabbed my purse, and went on with my day of craziness.

The kids got home from school and then it was the dinner rush and bedtime routine to take care of. After all was quiet and I was left to my own thoughts, I tried to wrap my brain around the fact that I would be taking my baby boy to Junior High the next day. That thought brought with it a fresh, new wave of anxiety and emotion and The Lump was quickly forgotten.

Four: DAY ONE

Sometimes in our lives we are inspired to do certain things. We don't always know why and feel like those things might be a bit odd, but we do them anyway because they just feel right. For me, one of those things was in the form of a little pink journal. That journal, along with my blog, was very therapeutic for me throughout my battle with cancer. I tried to keep a daily log of everything that happened. On day one (when I began writing in that journal) I had no idea that I would still be writing about my cancer journey after more than 1,000 days.

> *Day One: August 19, 2011*
> *"So today I joined the ranks of those who have cancer. It is still really weird to say it; even more so when I say it out loud." (Excerpt from my little pink journal.)*

And I said it out loud a lot, especially that first day. It was as if I had to constantly repeat it to have my brain register the fact that I had cancer.

Back to 8.19.11...

After dropping the cancer bomb on the love of my life and sending him back to his desk to try and resume a normal workday, I focused my attention on getting to Costco safely. I was trying to keep some sense of normalcy for my girls' sake, even though I was freaking out on the inside.

On my way to Costco, I called my mom. You know how when you are sick, the only thing you want is your mommy to take care of you? That is why I needed my mom at that moment. She couldn't answer the phone fast enough and before she could even say hello, I was a blubbering mess trying to get the words out of my mouth once again. "Mom, it's cancer. They found cancer!" Well, so much for sugar coating it for my girls.

The rest of the conversation with my mom consisted of her asking me a lot of questions that I just didn't have the answers to. I was crying. She was crying. My girls were crying. The first of many cry sessions had begun.

I finally reached my destination, told my mom that I would call her as soon as I had more information, and tried to gain some composure so I could get my shopping errand out of the way.

Normally I love a good trip to Costco, although my bank account does not. Costco sucks you in, like a black hole. You go in for milk and bread and come out with a cart full of stuff you just had to have, and hundreds of dollars poorer than when you went in. That day, however, I was sure that there would be no deterring from my list. I wanted to be in and out, possibly setting a record for spending the least amount of time inside a Costco.

As I was stepping out of the van, my phone rang again. It was my mother-in-law. Here was another great woman in my life that I knew I had to talk to right away. It was only about 15 years earlier that she had received the same devastating turn of events in her own life. She bravely endured surgeries and the worry that cancer brings, and had now been in remission for over ten years. I knew that she would be able to have perfect empathy for my situation.

"It's cancer," I told her. "I can't believe it, but they found cancer in my biopsy."

Cue tears again. I told her everything that I knew at that point, which wasn't much, and she told me she loved me and would immediately start praying for me.

In a fog, I fumbled my way into the store and somehow managed to wrangle all my girls and the necessary groceries. When I finally made it home, I had just enough time to dump the groceries onto the counter and head over to the elementary school to help with a back to school luncheon for the teachers.

When I arrived at the school, I was still stumbling around in my cancer diagnosis fog, which was getting thicker by the minute. I pretended that nothing was wrong and tried to put on a happy face. Because I had served the previous two years as PTA president, I had a lot of new PTA board members asking me for suggestions on some PTA related matters, but my insides were screaming. I wanted to shout at the top of my lungs, "I HAVE CANCER!" I felt as if yelling it would have released it from me. I was dying to tell my friends because I knew I would need every ounce of love and support that I could get my hands on, but I just could not find the right moment to drop the bomb.

Since there is never a perfect moment to tell someone that you have cancer, I decided that I needed to just rip the band aid off and break the news to some of my friends. Lyndsey and Cyndi happened to be the lucky ladies I talked to first. One of them asked me how my day was going and that triggered the eruption. My eyes filled up with tears and I felt the emotion of the morning rush to the surface.

"Not good, actually," I replied. "I just received a phone call telling me that I have breast cancer." (Insert expletives from Cyndi.)

The three of us hugged and cried and I replayed the whole morning for them. We ran into more of my friends and the hugging and crying started all over again. The whole moment was like an out-of-body experience.

When I was finished doing what I needed to do at the school and finally made it home for good, I found myself very restless. I was like a caged tiger, prowling around the house looking for something, anything, to get my mind off "the phone call." I picked up a few cluttered areas and then sat down to watch a movie with my girls.

As soon as I sat down, I just melted into the couch. I was drained, exhausted, and unable to move. My head was still reeling and trying to grasp everything. "How was I going to do this?" I thought. I had a family to raise, a husband to grow old with, people to help. This could not be happening to me.

What was I going to do now? Where was I supposed to even start? Fortunately, I was blessed with superb physicians from the very beginning of my journey and just as the helplessness of the situation started to overwhelm me, Dr. O'Neill called back with more information.

She said that she had been able to reach Dr. Mainwaring. Together they decided that they would get me scheduled for an MRI as soon as possible. They also agreed that Dr. Scott Leckman would be the perfect surgeon for my situation. They had even set up an appointment with him for the following Tuesday.

I was happy that things were moving rapidly. I felt like the sooner we could get this cancer out of me, the better. I wanted to move quickly so I could put it behind me. I was so naive. What I didn't realize in those beginning stages was that a cancer diagnosis does not use the words "quickly" or "putting it behind me" in reference to the process. It prefers words like "long", "life-altering", and "I'm here to stay."

The hospital was able to put me on the MRI schedule that very night. After checking in, I sat in the waiting room, held Mark's hand, and tried to untie the knots in my stomach.

When it was my turn, I got dressed in a very flattering hospital gown and headed down the longest hallway known to man. As I stepped into the room with the MRI machine, two very young, and might I add, very nice looking young men approached me. They looked too young to know much about breast MRI's, but then again, I was too young to be worried about a breast MRI, right? Their kindness surprised me and they made me feel extremely comfortable in the

24

situation. Well, as comfortable as one can feel when you are lying topless on a cold metal slab in front of two nice looking guys.

I had to lie on my stomach and position myself in a form that would allow my breasts to be photographed by the MRI machine. Once I was in the correct position, I had to remain perfectly still for 30 minutes. That was one of the longest 30 minutes of my life and not the most pleasant.

About 15 minutes into it every muscle in my body was screaming, "LET ME MOVE!" I felt that at any moment they were all going to rebel and I would start convulsing right there on that metal slab. So, I did the only thing that I could think to do. I started praying. I prayed that I would be able to stay still enough that they would be able to get the pictures they needed. I did not want to have to go through this process again. I also prayed that I would be able to feel calm and peaceful during the coming days as we discovered what we were dealing with.

"[I] feel drained and I can't think anymore. My plan is to keep a journal of this journey so that when I am done and tell my tale of being a survivor, I will be able to remember the details. I know that God will be with me on this journey. I know that it is in His plan for me and there is something I must learn from it."

Five: DAYS TWO & THREE

My first night with cancer was a very restless one. The unknowns pranced around in my head every time I closed my eyes. I finally woke up at about five o'clock in the morning and could not go back to sleep.

After trying to focus my attention on reading some scriptures, I realized that I needed to go to a place where I could shut the world out; a place where I could feel the peace and calm that my soul was longing to feel. For me, that place was the temple.

As a member of The Church of Jesus Christ of Latter-Day Saints, I have the opportunity to enter any one of our beautiful temples and perform sacred ordinances for people who have died. These people did not have the opportunity to perform the ordinances for themselves while they were alive. Although my service in the temple is on someone else's behalf, something remarkable happens to me while I am performing those acts of service; *I* am the one who ends up receiving a gift and blessing of peace and comfort.

I arrived at the Jordan River Temple bright and early that Saturday morning. As I participated in the temple work that day, I felt the love of my Father in Heaven. Tranquility flowed through me and I knew that whatever was in store for me, would be exactly what I needed so that I could learn and grow.

As I left the temple that day, I had a renewed sense of peace. Even though I felt in my heart that this was going to be a challenging load to bear, I knew that everything would be okay.

I also knew that I would forever be known as a breast cancer survivor and that my Father in Heaven would be looking out for me. I had already experienced so many small miracles and I felt the hope that there would be many more on the horizon. I was supposed to learn something from this experience and I trusted that God would lead me gently through the storm.

Confession time. I am a "worst case scenario" thinker. Whenever Mark goes out of town for business, I have thoughts of a fiery airplane crash or a head-on collision that would take him from me. I go through the whole thought process of, "*How could I function as a single parent full-time?*" and "*How would I ever survive without him?*"

Whenever one of my kids is sick, I am almost positive that they have some serious illness that would require surgery or hospitalization. I have been this way my whole life and sometimes it really stresses me out! Like, for instance, when you find out that you have cancer and suddenly every little ache or pain becomes a new source of stress and panic.

Even though I had felt such a calm reassurance that everything would be okay, my mind kept going over each little thing that was out of the ordinary. I had been having some headaches, which convinced me that the cancer had already made its way to my brain. I also felt like my right breast was a poisonous serpent. I just wanted to yank it off and throw it far away from me so it could not pump any more poison into my body.

One minute I was calm, with the thought, "*You are going to be just fine.*" The very next minute I was panicked, thinking, "*Nope. You're going to die".* It was exhausting going back and forth in my mind.

~ONE DAY AT A TIME~

The day after my trip to the temple was a Sunday and I found myself doing something that always lifted me up; attending my church meetings. At that time, I was serving in the presidency of our Primary, which is the organization for kids aged 18 months-11 years old.

There is something so wonderful about working with kids and teaching them about a loving God and His son, Jesus Christ. As I participated with them each week, I had my testimony strengthened just by hearing the children sing songs about our Savior and Redeemer. That Sunday I was looking forward to basking in the special spirit that often permeated the Primary room.

Before church started, I found our Relief Society* President to let her know of my diagnosis. Just like I knew that I would need the support of my family and friends, I also knew that I would need that same love and support from all the magnificent women in my ward.**

The Relief Society President and I slipped into a small classroom and I told her all that I knew about my situation. Then we hugged and cried. That was pretty much my life in the beginning stages of the journey, hugging and crying.

Word travels fast among women and as soon as our church services were over, I was immediately engulfed. There were people coming from every direction wanting to express their sorrow at hearing my news. They also pledged their support to help my family through our trial. That experience showed me how much the Lord truly loves us and how much he needs us to take care of each other here on earth.

I knew that all the women in my ward would be there to bring in meals, clean my house, take my children, and help me grocery shop. Whatever I needed, whatever my own family could not help with, they would be there to step in. It was a wonderful feeling to have that massive support system.

There is another important aspect to the gospel of Jesus Christ that I have utilized on numerous occasions throughout my life, including this particular period of time. It is having the priesthood, or the Lord's authority to act in His name, here on earth. Through this authority worthy priesthood holders can give special blessings to those who are in need.

28

That Sunday night, Mark and his dad gave me a blessing of strength and comfort. It was Mark who was speaking, but the words were coming from my Father in Heaven. I felt the burden of this diagnosis and all the unknowns, lifted, ever so slightly.

I came away from that blessing knowing that the road ahead was going to be very difficult and would require a lot of effort on my part. It was also confirmed to my soul that God was aware of my situation and that He loved me very much. I knew that He would be allowing some of my relatives, who were deceased, to be my angel companions during the coming months. They would be there to support me through the tough times that were to come. I was not going to have to go through this alone and I would have angels seen and unseen.

"It still feels very surreal. I am still trying to wrap my head around it. Two days ago, I was just another mom trying to make it through the day. Now I am a mom, with cancer, trying to kick its butt so I can do the things that Heavenly Father has in store for me."

*Relief Society is the organization for women in the Church of Jesus Christ of Latter-day Saints.
**A ward is our local congregation- much like a parish.

Six: DAY FIVE

After what felt like the longest weekend of my life, I was finally able to get some questions answered on day five. Unfortunately, I also had a hundred or so new, unanswered questions.

It was on that day that I met with my surgeon, Dr. Leckman. I could sense immediately that he was a kind man. I also felt that he was very knowledgeable about the surgeries that I would need and that he was an expert in his field. I would be in good hands. He made me feel completely at ease even though my heart was pounding out of my chest.

Mark was not able to come with me to meet with Dr. Leckman. He had a business trip that was scheduled months before our little world came crashing down and it could not be changed. So, I did the next best thing and took my mom to the appointment with me. We also called Mark and put him on speakerphone.

First, Dr. Leckman did a physical examination and took a brief history of what was going on. Then he shared with us the results of the MRI. It was not great news.

The MRI showed that the tumor measured about 29 mm, which was double the size that the ultrasound had shown. There was a little glimmer of hope when he said that, according to the MRI, there appeared to be nothing in my left breast. Whew. My lymph nodes looked clear as well. Double whew.

Dr. Leckman told me that I had Lobular Carcinoma, which meant that the cancer originated in the milk producing lobes of my breast. My cancer was a Grade 2 cancer. I had always heard about cancer *stages*, but had never heard of a cancer *grade*. The grade of the cancer basically tells you how aggressive it is. Since mine, at Grade 2, was smack dab in the middle, it wasn't super aggressive, but it wasn't going to just lie down and be lazy either.

There was really no way of knowing for sure how my cancer started. I was young. There was no known history of breast cancer in my family. I have since learned that 1 in every 8 women will be affected by breast cancer during their lifetime. 1 in 8!! That is a staggering statistic and it confirms in my mind that having a history of breast cancer is not your one and only risk factor. I also know that it doesn't really matter how old you are either. Breast cancer can happen to anyone, male or female, healthy or unhealthy. (*Here comes another plug for self-breast exams. You are not immune and of course you never think it's going to happen to you. Just do it anyway.*)

Now that we had some basic information about the tumor, we could proceed with some treatment options. However, before we could proceed too far, Dr. Leckman wanted to perform a gene test to determine if I was a carrier for either of the two known breast cancer genes, BRCA 1 or BRCA 2. I think it is safe to say that the gene test was the easiest part of this whole process. Just swish a little mouthwash around in your mouth and spit in a vial. That's it. Then it would be sent off to a lab to see if one of those gene mutations was lurking around in my system.

The nurse said that typically the gene test would take up to a month before the results would be back. *"A MONTH?"* my brain screamed. *"Are you kidding me?"* No way was I going to wait for a whole month. I needed answers now. Dr. Leckman assured me that he could have the results back in a week, two at the most. I guess a week was better than a month, but I was dying inside. It was not the time frame that I wanted to hear.

Why was this gene test so important, you might ask? Well, I basically had two options for a course of treatment. The option we chose would largely depend on the results of that test.

Option #1: If the gene test came back positive, saying that I was a carrier of either of the BRCA genes, then I would have to say goodbye to the "girls"--both of them, because having a breast cancer gene would make the probability of developing cancer in my other breast skyrocket. Having a double mastectomy would be the best option to prevent the cancer from showing up in my left breast. Also, as part of this treatment method, I would probably need a hysterectomy as well. Again, the BRCA genes are nasty and along with causing breast cancer, they could cause ovarian cancer as well. Needless to say, I was not too pleased with option numero uno.

Option #2: If the gene test came back negative, Dr. Leckman would start with a lumpectomy where he would remove the lump and some surrounding tissue. They would send the tumor and tissue to the lab to see if my margins were clear; or in layman's terms, to see if the cancer was in any of the surrounding tissue. Because a lobular carcinoma tumor likes to be tricky, this option would still leave me with the possibility of losing my entire right breast. I would have to do some radiation therapy with this option as well.

Both options would include the removal of some lymph nodes for testing. The pathology reports would tell us what stage my cancer was and if there was any cancer present in those lymph nodes. Depending on those results, we would know whether my treatment plan would include chemotherapy or some form of hormonal therapy.

> *"Wow--I really can't believe I am writing this in first person. I feel like I should be talking about someone else. It still doesn't feel totally real to me. I guess it won't feel real until surgery day."*

My mom and I left Dr. Leckman's office in stunned silence. There was so much information to digest and I was having a hard time swallowing it all. During

~DAY FIVE~

the next few days, I found it very hard to concentrate on anything, even simple tasks, like doing the dishes. I tried hard to keep myself occupied, but mostly I just felt like a ticking time bomb waiting to explode.

Seven: THE ROLLER COASTER RIDE

While I waited for the gene test results, I found myself stuck on a roller coaster ride of emotions. The fear and anxiety of all the unknowns sent me rushing downhill at an alarming speed. Then out of nowhere I would receive a tender mercy that would thrust me upwards to the crest of the next hill. That would allow me enough time to smile and catch my breath before careening down to the bottom again.

The emotional ride left me with a constant, throbbing ache in my head. I spent half of my time as a sobbing, blubbering mess. When I wasn't crying, I was trying to keep myself busy so that I wouldn't linger too long on all the possible outcomes that were roaming through my mind.

At times, I wondered if I had just been having a bad nightmare. I kept hoping that I would suddenly wake up and resume my normal life. After all, I didn't *look* sick. People who have cancer look sick, right? I didn't *feel* sick either. Other than some fatigue, I felt like I could run a marathon, or maybe a 5K. Yes, let's stick with a 5K. (I detest running.)

I did my best to try and NOT think about cancer, but found it impossible when every conversation I had with people started with, "Do you have any news?" "Nope, no news yet," I would have to report time and time again.

Day Nine: "I... am... exhausted. Emotionally, physically, spiritually--you name it. I am tapped out. I just keep trying to stay busy and keep a smile on my face, but today was hard. I snapped at my kids a lot...then I got angry with myself. Our lives could turn completely upside down in a few days. I should be making every moment count. But I couldn't today. I just couldn't put on the happy face anymore and unfortunately my family took the brunt of it. I'm sorry, guys. Tomorrow is another day. I will try to do better...I just want to cry all the time--cry because I'm scared, cry because I'm angry, [and] cry because I just want this nightmare to be over."

I became extremely impatient with the whole waiting process. I needed answers! Because I was a planner by nature, this cancer thing was really cramping my style. I couldn't move forward with any plans in my life, particularly the plans for my upcoming preschool year. (I taught preschool in my home.) My life was on hold and I did not like the music that was playing in the background.

As the days crept by and the turmoil in my heart grew, I started down a dangerous path of self-pity and despair. *"I don't want to do this!"* my mind screamed. *"What if I am not strong enough?"*

However, it seemed like every time I started down that dark path of self-pity, fear, and doubt, my faith in Jesus Christ steered me back in the right direction. I found myself craving more spirituality. I devoured my scriptures, prayed every single minute of the day, and scoured the Internet for words of comfort.

It was in those times of reflection that I received some of the most tender mercies. I was led to verses of scripture such as *"These things I have spoken unto you, that in me ye might have peace. In the world ye shall have tribulation: but be of good cheer; I have overcome the world." (John 16:33)*

Other tender mercies came in the form of earthly angels. My family and friends surrounded me in a bubble of love. Everywhere I turned I found someone giving me words of encouragement, sending me flowers, or bringing me food--lots and lots of food. That's one thing that we humans do when someone is suffering. We think of our favorite comfort foods and we share them. It's awesome. Especially when it involves chocolate.

My favorite earthly angel was my husband. When he came home from his business trip I felt like I could breathe again. It was so good to have him by my side. He was (and continues to be) the calm to my crazy and my reminder to take things one day at a time. Chemotherapy? Surgery? Radiation? Don't worry about it. We'll cross that bridge if and when we come to it.

He was right of course. Worrying would not change anything. The only thing that the worry was doing was causing me to lose precious hours of sleep, which, in turn, turned me into "grumpy mom." That was when I decided that I needed to find a place of peace and harmony within myself and ditch the roller coaster ride for good.

Eight: DAYS 13, 14, & 15

My moment of clarity and peace came during the morning of Day Thirteen. It had been eight days since my appointment with Dr. Leckman and I had not heard anything in the way of results. I was not looking forward to another day of the unknown.

But in those wee hours of the morning when the house was still, I reached the conclusion that I had been searching for: I needed to stop living each day under the rule of my anxiety and fear. No amount of apprehension was going to make the test results come back faster. Worrying would not change anything and it would not make the cancer go away.

What caused this great shift in my thought process? While reading in "The Book of Mormon" that morning, I had the impression to go to LDS.org and search for articles that spoke about finding peace. As I filtered through the results, I felt compelled to read two of them.

The first was a talk by Lance B. Wickman entitled <u>But If Not.</u>* One quote seemed to jump off the page at me.

"Mortality's supreme test is to face the 'why' and then let it go, trusting humbly in the Lord's promise that 'all things must come to pass in their time."

Okay. Face the why and then let it go.

The second article was a talk given by Elder Quentin L. Cook.** Again, there was a section that penetrated my heart as I was reading.

"I testify that the Atonement of Jesus Christ covers all of the trials and hardships that any of us will encounter in this life. At times when we may feel to say, 'Hope you know, I had a hard time', we can be assured that He is there and we are safe in His loving arms."

The words of those two articles combined with the words of scripture all came together with one resounding thought in my mind. It was as though my Father in Heaven was saying to me, "Relax! It's going to be okay!"

For the rest of that day, tranquility surged through my veins. I felt like the old me again. I was on a spiritual high. Day 13= very good day. Day 14= not so much.

After feeling so peaceful on Day 13, I felt like I could conquer anything. Then as Day 14 progressed, the despair and anger that I had so gently pushed out of my brain started to creep back in. My resolve to be calm, cool, and collected lasted about as long as my determination to not have piles of stuff on my kitchen counter.

It had now been nine days since my appointment and there was still no news about the gene test. I was more restless than ever and yet, I could not make myself get up off the couch and accomplish anything noteworthy. Then I got mad at myself for wasting time. I guess my roller coaster ride wasn't over after all.

By the time Day 15 rolled around, I didn't know how I was going to be able to pull myself through another day of waiting. I felt like my life was on the line and with each day that passed I grew more desperate. I needed answers so I could move forward and get this cancer out of me.

"I didn't get a call this morning and I couldn't get anyone to answer at Dr. Leckman's office--so I called his cell phone. I felt bad to do that, but I am in desperation mode here! He put his secretary to work calling the gene place. After my conversation with him, I panicked...What if I have chosen the wrong doctor to help me through this?

Well, I lost it. I sobbed, begging, and pleading to my Father in Heaven to give me some sort of confirmation to know I was taking the right path. At that moment of complete desperation, I felt it--God's love for me...I was calm.

I know that my Father is there, that He loves me and is crying with me. I know that He has led me to these good doctors who are going to help me through this. I know that I am in His hands. I am His child and He is aware of my struggles."

I sat on the floor with tear stained cheeks. My body shuttered as it recovered from 20 minutes of a sobbing session worthy of an award. My head was pounding, but my mind felt calm. All the fear and worry had left. In its place was the calm reassurance that everything would be all right. I wondered how many more times God was going to have to calm the raging storm inside me before I actually started believing in His promises?

*Lance B. Wickman, "But If Not," *Ensign,* Nov. 2002, 30.
**Quentin L. Cook, "Hope Ya Know, We Had a Hard Time," LDS General Conference October 2008.

Nine: THE WAITING GAME

The days continued to roll slowly by. By mid-afternoon on Day 19 I couldn't take it any longer. I had to know those gene test results! The anxiety of waiting and wondering was more than I could bear. I grabbed my cell phone and dialed Dr. Leckman's office.

"I'm so sorry," the nurse said. "The test results have to be delivered by FedEx and we have not seen the deliveryman yet today. Let me call the gene testing lab to make sure they have sent the results."

"Yes, please do, and thank you," I said through gritted teeth.

Soon after that phone call, I received a call from a plastic surgeon's office asking me if they could schedule a "get to know you" appointment for the following week.

"Well, I don't think that next week is going to work," I said. "I am hoping to have surgery at the end of this week."

Now, I still had no idea whether I would be having surgery, but I felt that if I said it out loud, the universe would hear it and somehow make it happen.

"Okay," the nurse replied. "Let me check with Dr. Leckman's office and get back to you then."

~THE WAITING GAME~

My frustration level had reached its max. I felt like I kept taking one step forward and three gigantic steps back. A few, painfully long hours ticked by and then suddenly my phone started to ring. I snatched it up, hoping to finally hear some good news.

"I am so sorry to have to tell you this," said Dr. Leckman's nurse, "but I have been chasing a bunch of people at the gene testing lab and found out that because of Labor Day, the test will not be delivered until tomorrow. Also, Dr. Leckman does not want to move forward until we have those results. He is suggesting that we hold off on scheduling something with the plastic surgeon until we see the results and make our final plans."

I was in disbelief. I said thank you and hung up my phone. Then the rage set in. I was angry that the test results were not in and that my life would continue to be on hold. I was also angry that I had postponed starting preschool. Now that I would not be having surgery at the end of the week, I realized that I could have stuck with my original plans and started at the beginning of the school year.

The biggest source of my anger was that I was just plain tired of talking about, thinking about, and wondering about the cancer. I could not be strong on the outside anymore while my insides were slowly crumbling away.

The hardest part about this whole situation was that there was absolutely no one to blame. There also wasn't anyone or anything to take my anger out on, except for my phone, which I threw to the floor.

I followed my poor phone and sank to my knees, unable to make myself do anything but sit there and feel sorry for myself. Unsure of what to do next, I wore out a spot on the carpet as I stomped back and forth, letting the anger and frustration boil over.

I sat down at the computer to write a blog entry, pounding the keys until my fingers hurt. There! Take that computer keyboard! I also took a gander at Facebook and it was while reading posts there, that I noticed a strange pattern emerging. Almost every post that I read expressed the writer's frustration about how he/she was waiting for something.

It was then that I realized, or rather, the Lord tenderly pounded a message into my brain. Yes, I was playing the waiting game, but it was a game that people everywhere must play for various reasons.

For some, the game is the agonizing wait to start a family either because of infertility or the adoption process. For others, it is waiting to hear back from a job interview after they have been out of work for months. Whatever the reason, people have to wait.

I was not alone in my misery and I would not have to wait forever. Eventually I would be having surgery and the bottom line was, we would be moving forward. But for now, I just needed to heed my own advice and "take a chill pill." (This is a phrase my kids hear from me on a regular basis.)

As I felt the rage subsiding, I heard a knock on the door. I opened it to find my mother-in-law standing there. She had come to see how I was holding up. I filled her in on the situation and she left me with a hug and some words of wisdom.

"From now on you just need to wake up every day and think, 'Okay, normally I would be doing preschool or PTA stuff or whatever, but I'm not and that is alright. Now, what fun thing am I going to fill that time with instead?' You can do this," she said.

Okay. I get it. I will stop throwing my "I can't be in control and I don't like it" tantrum and make the most of this time that I have while I am feeling healthy and strong.

Later that night as I was pondering this distressing situation that I was in, I realized that eventually the waiting game would come to an end. I had no idea when that would be, but I would just have to settle in and endure the wait well. By keeping a tight grip on my faith in God's plan for me, I knew I would be able to make it.

Ten: THE GOOD NEWS

Finally, on Day 20, my waiting game came to an end. However, I had just about given up hope for the day. It was after 4:30 in the afternoon and I still had not heard anything from Dr. Leckman's office. I spoke with Mark on the phone and told him that it looked like we would have to wait yet another day.

Suddenly, the most glorious thing appeared on my caller ID—Dr. Leckman's number. I had not been that happy to see someone's name on my caller ID since Mark and I were dating.

Just as I was about to answer the call, I felt my old friend, Panic, start tapping on my brain. Even though I had endured such a painful waiting game and was looking forward to some answers, I wasn't sure that I wanted to face the reality that this conversation would bring. I waited until the last possible moment before answering the call.

"Hello?" I said tentatively.

"Desirae? Dr. Leckman here. I have some very good news for you."

"Really?" I squeaked. Please say that this has all been a big joke and I really don't have cancer. That would be the best news ever.

"Yes," he replied, "the gene testing came back negative. This is really good news and it means that you are an excellent candidate for a lumpectomy. When would you like to schedule that procedure?"

Umm--let's see. How about yesterday? Does that work? No? Okay, I will settle for Friday then. Finally, 20 days into this nightmare, I felt like I could take a giant leap forward.

I hung up the phone with a plan, which is what I had been craving. I was not completely out of the woods yet, but I was definitely going to take the small victory of the gene test being negative. Although there was still a good possibility that we could be dealing with more than just the one tumor or the presence of cancer in my lymph nodes, I was going to take this good news and run with it. I didn't know how many other "good news" phone calls I was going to get.

Day 22 dawned bright and clear. It was a good day for surgery. I was ready to have the lumpy invader taken out of me so I could move on with life and put this whole cancer episode far behind me.

After checking in at the surgical center, they sent me to radiology so that I could have an isotope injected into my tumor site. That was the first step in a procedure called a Sentinel Lymph Node Biopsy.

Through use of an ultrasound, the radiologist injected a metallic isotope into my tumor. It would take about an hour for the isotope to travel from my tumor to my lymph nodes. While in surgery, my doctor would sweep a metal detector type of device over my lymph nodes to determine where the isotope was. That would allow him to take only the "sentinel lymph nodes" or the lymph nodes where the cancer would have traveled to first.

The benefit of that procedure was that instead of making a large incision and taking out a huge cluster of lymph nodes, Dr. Leckman would be able to make a much smaller incision and take out a minimal number of nodes. This would greatly reduce the risk of getting lymphedema (which I will explain later) and leave me with smaller scars.

When I was done in the radiology department, I was taken to a waiting room back in the surgical center. While waiting for my turn for surgery, my phone kept buzzing. The day before, I had issued my blog followers a challenge. "Pink Friday" it would be called. I had grand visions of the beautiful scrapbook that I would make when my journey was through and to do that, I would need pictures.

I encouraged everyone to send me a picture of them wearing pink. I figured that for sure, my family would participate and maybe even a few of my closest friends. I was astonished to see that with each buzz of my phone, another picture of someone dressed in pink was being sent to me. There were pictures of my family and close friends, but I was amazed to see that there were also pictures of acquaintances, people that I hadn't seen since high school, friends of friends, and co-workers of family members. The list went on and on and I was overwhelmed with all the love that was being sent to me in digital form.

"I have over 30 pictures so far and I know that I will be getting a few more. It is very humbling. I cannot believe all these people love me so much. People that I have not seen in so many years and people that I have never even met. I feel so blessed to have all of these wonderful people in my life."

When the time came to head back to surgery, I kissed Mark goodbye and ventured down a hallway that, unfortunately, I would come to know very well.

I climbed up on the surgical bed and tried to calm the zillion butterflies that were flying around in my tummy. The nurses bustled about the operating room, prepping me and the instruments that Dr. Leckman would use to remove my lumpy invader. I recall focusing my gaze on the glaring surgical light above me as I slowly drifted off to a land where cancer was not an issue.

The next thing I knew, I was in the recovery room chatting it up with the nurses. As soon as I was stable, Mark gathered me up and we headed home. I spent the rest of the day in my bed, watching TV and nodding off every hour or so as the anesthesia worked its way out of my system.

The next day was spent lounging around and taking it easy. I felt good as long as I kept up on my pain medications and had an ice pack handy. Everything was going relatively well until I took off the bandages and had my first look at the new me.

> *"I didn't think I would have a problem with how my breast would look. After all, they just took a small tumor out, right? [Once I removed the bandages] I was able to see the incision and everything for the first time. Wow--was not expecting such a big incision. It's probably a good two inches long at least. I guess this is good. Dr. Leckman says he usually has to make two incisions: one for the tumor and one for the lymph node removal...I was also able to see that I am missing some 'plumpness' on top now. I really didn't think it would bother me, but it was kind of a shock...However, I have to say that Mark gave it an appropriate nickname--'Frankenboob'. He can always make me laugh. Love you, honey."*

Now that the lumpectomy portion of this journey was complete, it was time to do some more waiting. Dr. Leckman sent the tumor and lymph nodes to the pathology lab. About four days after my surgery I saw Dr. Leckman's number on my caller ID again. As I reached over to answer it I started pleading inside my head.

"Please, oh please, let it be another 'good news' phone call."

Eleven: WORST-CASE SCENARIO, ANYONE?

Dr. Leckman asked if Mark and I could meet him at his office that afternoon. Uh-oh. Something told me that my good news moments would not be continuing. All the years I had spent going over various worst-case scenarios in my mind was finally catching up with me. Here we were, on Day 26, smack dab in the middle of worst-case scenario land.

I was nervous the whole morning, but as the time for our appointment drew closer, my nervousness slowly disappeared and was replaced by a strange feeling of perfect calmness.

In my heart, I knew that I would be receiving some pretty bad news, so when this calm feeling washed over me, I was confused. I had been in so much agony thinking about the worst things imaginable. So why wasn't I continuing my freak-out sessions? Why was I not a basket case of worry anymore? Apparently, God had other plans for me and He placed me in a protective bubble. Any negative thoughts that tried to penetrate the thin, filmy surface of my bubble just bounced back into the universe.

"As this whole thing has progressed, I have never been able to pray for the easiest road. I have only been able to pray that I may be prepared to accept the test and the road that lies ahead. Today I felt that preparation."

At the appointment, Mark and I sat together, hand in hand. Dr. Leckman sat across from us. His kind face smiled with compassion as he shared with us the news we had feared from the very beginning.

During the lumpectomy surgery, Dr. Leckman discovered that the tumor was much bigger than even the MRI had shown. In fact, it wasn't really a solid mass of a tumor at all. It was more like a spider web creeping about all over the place and the pathology report told us that there was cancer present in the lymph nodes that were removed.

For a moment, my mind went numb as I listened to him share the information with us. I was waiting for the fear to grab hold of my heart, but it never came. There were angels present in that room that day. I know it. I felt it. My Grandpa Holt, my Uncle Ray, and other relatives were there, holding me together. The Spirit of the Lord was also there helping my mind to stay open and free from negative thoughts so that I could soak in and comprehend all the information the doctor was sharing with me.

Dr. Leckman told us that he had set up an appointment for the next afternoon with Dr. Chandramouli, an oncologist with the Utah Cancer Specialists. We thanked him for taking such good care of me and for attending to all the little details.

He must have sensed the apprehension that continued to plague my aura so he kindly took a moment to share his educated opinion of what might happen next. He said that I would most definitely need to have a mastectomy since my tumor was not a solid mass but rather a tumor with wispy tentacles. We couldn't be sure that the lumpectomy took care of the entire tumor that was twisting and winding around my breast tissue. I would have the choice between a unilateral (just the remainder of my right breast) or a bilateral (both breasts) mastectomy.

He also said that I had a couple of other factors that would probably push me into chemotherapy and radiation land. The first factor was my age. I was only 33 years old, which is young to be diagnosed with breast cancer. When someone my age does end up with cancer, it usually is a very aggressive cancer. That meant that whatever treatment options we discussed would need to be very aggressive so that we could "fight fire with fire." The second factor was the fact that the cancer was present in my lymph nodes, which meant there was a high possibility of it being somewhere else in my body.

Mark and I walked to the car in silence, trying to process all the information we had just received. My heart was hurting just thinking about the conversation I would have to have with my children. The road we were about to travel was going to be a very difficult road for everyone in our family. I thought, and Mark agreed, that it would be better to wait until after we met with the oncologist before we talked to the kids about everything that was going on. That way, they would know the actual plan instead of our speculated one.

On Day 27, I met my oncologist for the first time. Wow. I actually have an oncologist. How did that happen? Up to that point in my journey, I had been blessed with amazing doctors. Could that trend possibly continue? Would I love him and feel confident in his care? Or would I hate him and have to hurry and find someone else? That would have been awful because finding a new doctor would have meant more waiting.

"Oh, I hope that this doctor will be just as amazing as my other doctors," I said in my mind.

From the moment Dr. Chandramouli sauntered into the room, I knew that we were in the right place. He shook our hands and I immediately felt comfortable in his presence. It was another tender mercy.

Dr. C. reviewed all the things that we had gone over with Dr. Leckman. Then he got down to the nitty gritty--the stage of my cancer and my treatment options.

"He pretty much confirmed the fact that this is bad. He defined it as Stage 3B breast cancer which freaked me out...a lot."

Stage 3. How in the world did we go from "it's probably just a fibroid" to Stage 3 breast cancer? To say that I was stunned would be a huge understatement.

Here's the definition of Stage 3 breast cancer from the National Breast Cancer Foundation's website:

"Stage 3 cancer means that the breast cancer has extended to beyond the immediate region of the tumor and may have invaded nearby lymph nodes and muscles, but has not spread to distant organs. Although this stage is considered to be advanced, there are a growing number of effective treatment options. This stage is divided into three groups: Stage 3A, Stage 3B, and Stage 3C. The difference is determined by the size of the tumor and whether the cancer has spread to the lymph nodes and surrounding tissue."*

It was at that point in the conversation that Dr. Chandramouli had to step out of the room for a few moments. After he left, I looked at Mark and neither of us could contain the tears any longer. We were in shock. To hear the words "Stage 3 cancer" took the wind right out of our sails. We were both familiar enough with cancer stages to know that there was only one more stage after Stage 3 and then you are gone. We only had a few minutes to gather our composure before the doctor came back in so we could discuss my treatment options.

I have always been somewhat of an overachiever. I like to go the second mile like the Primary Song** suggests. But goodness gracious! Did I really have to carry that over into every aspect of my life? This was not just going to be a simple surgery and "move on with your life" kind of deal.

Nope. I was going to feast on the all-you-can-eat buffet of breast cancer treatments; sampling a little bit of everything, if you will.

~WORST-CASE SCENARIO, ANYONE?~

Course #1 would include two tests--an EKG (electrocardiogram) and a PET (Positron Emission Tomography) scan. I needed to have an EKG because one of the chemo meds I would need was known for causing heart problems later on down the road. My doctor wanted to have a baseline EKG just in case the drug decided to wreak havoc on my heart. I also needed to have a PET scan so we would know if the cancer was lurking anywhere else in my body.

For Course #2 I would need to have another outpatient surgery to have a PORT-A-CATH placed under my skin, just below my collarbone. Commonly known as a "port", this small medical appliance would have a catheter attached to it that would feed directly into a vein in my neck. That way, when I went in for my chemo treatments, I would not have to get an IV every time. The nurses could access my port and administer the drugs through it, saving the veins in my arms.

During Course #3 of my smorgasbord, I would begin chemo treatments. That would happen after I had recovered from my lumpectomy and port surgeries. My first chemo drugs would be a concoction affectionately known as "The Red Devil." Its official name is Adriamycin Cytoxan. (Say that fast five times.) I would come to find out that it does indeed live up to its name, but more on those good times later.

After finishing four rounds of the A/C chemo, I would have another PET scan to see if the chemo was working. Then I would begin my second chemo drug, Taxotere. That one would not be as horrific as the A/C, but it would pack a powerful punch of side effects nonetheless.

For Course #4 we would move on to the mastectomy portion of my treatment schedule. As I mentioned before, I would have to choose between losing one breast or both breasts. In some respects, it would have been easier to have the gene test come back positive because then it wouldn't have been a choice; they would have said that both breasts would have to go. As it was, I had a huge decision to make, and it took many hours of pondering, fasting, and praying to determine which one to choose.

To round out the meal for Course #5, I would need to have twenty-five radiation treatments followed by reconstruction surgery (if I did, in fact, choose to have reconstruction.)

Check please, and I won't be leaving a tip.

"Welcome to Hell. I read an article where the author said that we will have times in our lives where we will want to beg the Father to 'let this cup pass.' This is definitely that time for me. I know that I can do this. I just don't want to do this. I'm scared to find out what turns up on the PET scan. I can deal with this in my lymph nodes and breast. I can even deal with it if it has spread a little. But please, oh please don't let it be in my brain or liver. Please let me have a chance to fight this. I try not to worry about dying, but the past two days have been hard. It is way more serious than anyone anticipated. I am not going to give up. I will fight this until the bitter end for sure. It's just turning out to be a harder battle than I thought it was going to be. I hope I have the strength to get through it."

We left the doctor's office that day with a growing sense of dread settling deep into our bones. Now we had to face the unpleasant task of filling the kiddos in on what the next few months of our lives would entail.

After dinner that night, we gathered everyone together in the living room. I don't remember my exact words, but I can vividly see the image of their faces in my mind. They displayed looks of shock, terror, fear, and sadness.

They took the news as well as could be expected and we all shed a fair number of tears. Because Josh and Emma were older, their tears came from a limited understanding of the severity of the situation. Abbie and Ellie were crying mostly because everyone else was crying. At their tender ages, they did not understand the concept of cancer. However, they could feel the anxiety, fear, and sadness that invaded our happy home.

It tore me up inside to be so brutally honest about the situation, but I knew that I could not sugar coat things for them. I am a talker. I like to talk about lots of things and I knew that I would not be silent during this cancer journey. I did

52

not want to share any information with a family member or friend that I had not already shared with my kids. They needed to hear everything from me and I needed them to know that I was an open book. If they had a question or concern, they were to ask me right away. No letting things fester. No unnecessary worrying. We were in this fight together. I was the one who would be having the surgeries and treatments, but it was a battle that was going to affect all of us.

*"What Does It Mean to Have Stage 3 Breast Cancer?", Retrieved from www.nationalbreastcancer.org/breast-cancer-stage-3
**"Go the Second Mile". *Children's Songbook,* 167

Twelve: PREPARING FOR THE RED DEVIL

Chemotherapy. The very word sends shivers down my spine as I think about all that it entails. For most people, the only experience they have with chemo is what they have seen portrayed in the movies or on television. For others, they have watched helplessly as a loved one travels down the long chemo road. For a select number of us, we have the unfortunate opportunity to speak about chemotherapy in first person. I never thought I would be included in that group of people.

It felt strange to be throwing around the words, "chemotherapy", "mastectomy", and "radiation." It felt even stranger the closer I got to my actual chemo start date. I was dreading it and anticipating it at the same time. Dreading it because I did not want to have to endure the side effects that I had heard about. Anticipating it because I knew that chemo was not the real enemy. Hopefully, it would be killing the real enemy.

I don't think one can truly prepare for chemotherapy. It's like trying to prepare for a baby. You read all the books. You talk to people who have been there.

~PREPARING FOR THE RED DEVIL~

You buy all the stuff you think you may need. You think you are set. Then it happens and you realize just how unprepared you are.

I really had no idea what to expect. I did as much homework as I could. Mark and I attended a chemo information class at the cancer center.

I talked to my Aunt Cheri and others who were chemo/cancer survivors. I scoured the Internet and read all the things that I could that pertained to breast cancer chemotherapy treatments.

I knew as much as I could know. The problem now was waiting to see exactly how the chemo would affect me. Every cancer diagnosis is unique and everyone's chemo experience is a little different. What was a problem for my Aunt Cheri may not be a problem for me and vice versa. We would just have to wait and see how my body decided to react to the poison.

Fortunately, I had some things to keep me busy as my "C" day (chemo day) drew nearer. I had been able to start my preschool classes not long after my lumpectomy surgery. That was a huge relief because it brought a sense of normalcy to my crazy existence. The kids in my two classes were going to be very therapeutic for me. I could already see that the choice to not teach during my cancer journey was not a choice at all. I would need that job to get me out of bed every morning.

My job as a mother was another thing that was keeping me busy and helping me persevere through this trial. I tried to focus on my children's needs and help them as much as possible. There was homework to do and activities to be shuttled to. I was also trying to make sure that people were lined up to take my place as taxi driver during the times that I would be unavailable.

I had many great conversations with my kiddos during that time of waiting and I could see that cancer was starting to make some positive changes in our lives, not just negative ones. One of those positive changes was that the cancer was forcing me to slow down. I was calmer, nicer, and less stressed about all the little things that used to drive me crazy. I was more in tune with the important things and I was taking the time to enjoy every moment that life had to offer.

"Last night as I was putting the girls to bed, Emma said, 'You're the best mom ever!' I told her thank you and then Abbie said, 'Yeah, you've been really nice since you got cancer. You hardly yell at all!' Ha! What a silly girl. I guess I have been too preoccupied with trying to stay alive that all of the little things haven't bugged me as much. I hope that this is something that will be included in the 'new & improved' Des--less yelling and being a nicer mom. I would love that. I hate when I yell all the time."

Another part of my chemo preparation included a new hairstyle. I had been growing my hair out for a few years and it currently was the longest I had ever had. I loved my hair. It was devastating for me to think of losing it all and I thought that maybe it would be a little easier to lose it if I let it go a little at a time. That's where my sister-in-law, Julie, stepped in to help.

Our original plan was for me to go to her house and have my hair cut into a cute, short, bob style. The morning of my appointment, I had the thought that it might be fun to have her put a couple of pink streaks in my hair. I had never done anything quite that daring with my hair (although there have been some pretty amazing hairstyles in my hair history.) I sent Julie a text to see if she had any pink hair coloring and if she would be willing to do some pink streaks. She called me back with an even better idea.

"What if we have a pink party and all the girls put some pink in their hair?" she said.

"That sounds like a great plan!" I said. "Count us in!"

That night all the Ogden girls gathered at my in-law's house for a party of pink proportions. My mother-in-law made her famous rolls with a hint of pink food coloring. My sister-in-law, Michelle, made some delicious raspberry ice cream complete with a sign that read, "I Scream for a Cure." The dinner was so much fun and afterwards I got spoiled with hats and scarves and lots of love.

After I opened my gifts, we all gathered together in my mother-in-law's beauty shop. It was crowded, crazy, and so much fun. Almost everyone added a little pink to their hair that night, including my girls. They were so excited to be included in this pink adventure.

I was the last one in the chair and by the time Julie was done, I felt like a new woman, complete with two pink streaks and a super sassy cut. That night brought me one step closer to facing the things that were just over the horizon and it was exactly what my hurting heart needed.

On Day 39, I found myself checking in at the outpatient surgical center once again. This time I would be leaving with a lump instead of losing one. It was time for my PORT-A-CATH placement.

Everything went smoothly with the placement, although the procedure was a little more involved than I thought it would be. I had been feeling calm during the days before the surgery, but I guess the anxiety was still slinking around in my body, because when I came out of the anesthesia, I just cried and cried and could not stop.

The recovery nurse was very sweet and tried to help me get my mind off things by asking me questions about my kids. As I talked about my munchkins, I started to calm down and the tears eventually stopped. I finally shook off enough of the anesthesia that they told me it was time to pack up and head home.

When we got home, the exhaustion of everything took over and I was out like a light. The port site was sore, but as long as I took my pain meds, I felt okay.

"Overall, I feel so calm. Really. It is weird. But I know without a shadow of a doubt that it is all of the prayers, good wishes, and sweet words of encouragement [that is making me feel so calm.]

It is the loving arms of my Savior as He is taking [me by the hand] and helping me through this burden. I love that I have my Savior and my Father in heaven to help me through this. It makes all the difference in the world."

Thirteen:

BATTLING THE RED DEVIL

I woke up the morning of my first chemo treatment with a "heart attack", on my front porch. My amazing neighbors got together and plastered our door and porch area with dozens of paper hearts. The hearts were filled with notes of love and encouragement. It was the perfect way to start a day that would be filled with uncertainty and worry.

We arrived at the cancer center shortly before lunchtime. The first step was to have one of the nurses access my port. I still had the bandage on from the surgery so I had not actually seen what the area around my port looked like yet. Truth be told, once the nurse took the bandage off, I was a tiny bit freaked out. It looked like something from an extra-terrestrial world was trying to burst through my skin.

Normally I would have been able to use some numbing cream on the skin around my port on the days that it would be accessed. But because it had been bandaged, I had not been able to use the cream. That made the poking and prodding process of accessing the port a little painful, especially since it was still a little on the sore side from the port placement surgery. Plus, it was a new process for me so I was a little on the tense side, which I am sure added to the discomfort.

To access my port, the nurse gently pushed an IV needle through the tender skin by my collarbone and into the center of the port. There was a thin line of tubing attached to the needle. Once the needle was secured with medical tape, the tubing rested gently on top of my shirt.

When it was time to administer the chemo meds, the nurse would be able to attach the IV fluids to this thin line of tubing and the medication would flow directly into the vein in my neck. The port could also be used to take blood, which was handy because I would need to have my blood tested every time I had an appointment.

Once the port was situated and my blood was being checked, the nurse took us to a consultation room to wait to talk with Dr. Chandramouli. Up to that point of the day, I had been able to keep myself busy and there was no time for the anxiety to kick in. Now that I was sitting in this room, surrounded by silence, the anxiety came rushing in all at once.

Not only would I begin chemo this day, but I would also be getting my PET scan results. It was the moment I had been waiting for since first hearing the words, "You have cancer." I would now be able to know for sure if the cancer made its way to other parts of my body and that left me short of breath and lightheaded. Like a fish caught in a whirlpool, the thoughts in my head swirled around and around. *"Had the cancer already started destroying other organs in my body?"* *"Did we catch it in time?"* *"Was the PET scan able to see all of the tumors invading my body?"* The tension in the air was palpable and the suspense was almost more than I could stand.

"Good news," Dr. C said, as he came into the room. "The PET scan report looks good. No cancer anywhere else. Now, the PET scan can only pick up cancer that is over 5mm in size, so there could be some little floater cells out there, but the chemo will most likely kill all of those."

I had to fight to keep from sliding off my chair and onto my knees. The sense of relief was overwhelming. That was very good news indeed. Now I really felt like I could hit this head on, guns a-blazing.

After Dr. C. gave us a few more words of instruction, he sent me and Mark to the "chemo staging area." (Those are just fancy words for another waiting room, because cancer = waiting.)

Once my nurse was ready for me, she led me back to a room filled with recliner chairs. Sounds comfy, right? Sure, if by comfy you mean sitting in a recliner and being filled to the brim with a few different poisons. I chose the first open chair that I came to and settled in for the next part of this nightmare.

My nurse was truly delightful, which I was grateful for. She took the time to explain everything that she was going to do and made sure that Mark and I understood the process. She was extremely positive and upbeat and she made sure that I was feeling as comfortable as possible.

She got my port line hooked up to the IV bag and started me on my pre-meds which consisted of some anti-nausea medication and some steroids. The anti-nausea meds would hopefully get a jump-start on controlling that aspect of chemo side effects while the steroids would help prevent an allergic reaction to the chemo.

Once everything was flowing, it was time to sit back and relax, or try and relax. It wasn't exactly the most relaxing position to be in. As I looked at the patients around me, I could see that they were all in various stages of treatment.

Some already had no hair. Others showed promise of new hair with a head full of fuzz. Some had a bin close by just in case they needed to vomit mid-treatment. Most of them were much older than me. There was a gentleman who looked like he was probably close to my age, but for the most part, I was the baby of the bunch.

Tell me again how I got here? Wasn't I supposed to be enjoying my life as a young mother; running her kids to and fro, baking cookies, volunteering at the school, and doing all the other things that young moms do?

Yes, that was what I should have been doing. Instead, I was in a cancer treatment center, sitting in a slightly comfortable recliner, with medications running through my veins. I felt a little light-headed as my brain tried to sort through that was happening to me. Amid my small panic attack, I received a text. Thankful for the distraction, I checked to see whom it was from. What I saw on my phone, I will never forget.

It was a text from my PTA friend, Lyndsey. In that text, she included a picture of the entire staff and student body at Liberty Elementary. Almost everyone was wearing something pink. The tears rolled down my cheeks. I could not believe that so many people cared that much about me. It was an incredible opportunity for me to have that kind of demonstration of love. I felt, and still feel, very fortunate to have experienced it.

Armed now with a huge surge of love and support, I was able to pull myself out of the panic attack and just enjoy the time that I was able to spend with Mark. It was our first chemo date. Of course, we were not alone in the room and it was not the kind of date that I preferred, but a date is a date, even if that date includes killing cancer.

Once the pre-meds were done, it was time to bring in the big guns; the "Red Devil." They were not kidding about the red color. That chemo was the brightest red I had ever seen, like a neon cherry Kool-Aid.

The Adriamycin chemo could not be administered through a regular IV bag. Instead, my nurse would have to push it through a syringe--two of them in fact. As she was getting everything ready, she handed me a cup of ice.

"Why don't you start chewing on this ice," she said. "If you can keep your mouth cold while I am administering the chemo, it should prevent you from getting mouth sores."

Yes, of course! Give me all the ice you can get your hands on! Mouth sores did not sound pleasant and chewing on ice was something I could definitely handle. As I took a mouthful and began to chew away, my nurse started suiting up in her armor. It was not a real suit of armor of course, but in order to administer the Adriamycin chemo, she had to put a hazardous waste uniform on over her clothes.

Whoa. Back up a minute. Let me get this straight. You are going to now inject a screaming red liquid poison into my delicate veins, but you can't do that unless you are wearing a HAZMAT suit? How was it not just going to kill me outright? Something about that scenario was not right.

Once my nurse was situated and safe, it was go-time. She started with the first syringe. I watched as the syringe plunger slowly pushed the poison into my IV line. While she was administering it, she explained the need for the special outfit. If the Adriamycin chemo were to get on your skin at all, it would eat right through it. Sounds like fun. I guess it had to be tough to kill cancer, but eating through your skin? Yikes!

Then she went over some safety protocol that I would need to do at home. One of the first side effects that I would notice would be red urine. I would need to make sure that I flushed the toilet immediately after using it and not get any urine on the toilet seat. Ok, no pressure; it's only red pee that can eat your flesh. That's not a problem, is it? Man, things just kept getting better and better.

After both syringes were empty, and the Red Devil was coursing through my veins, it was time to administer chemo med #2--Cytoxan. That one could be administered through an IV bag, so it wasn't as scary. However, as soon as my nurse started the pump, I felt a rush of pain in my sinus area and experienced one of the worst sinus headaches I had ever had. She saw me reach up and grab the bridge of my nose.

"Are you having sinus pain?" she asked.

"Yes, you could say that," I moaned.

"Well, let me slow the flow down then. Sometimes if we have it go slowly, then we can avoid causing the sinus pain."

Yes, please, and thank you. As soon as it slowed down, the sinus pain subsided and I could somewhat relax again. Once that IV bag was empty, the nurse flushed my port with saline and I was free to go. Just like that, my first round of chemo was done.

I wasn't quite sure what to expect once I got home. Would I be nauseous? Actively throwing up? Achy? Only time would tell. I felt okay for the first few hours. After dinner, the nausea kicked in so I took some meds and went to bed early.

The following day, I had to go back to the cancer center so I could receive a Neulasta shot. Just a little side note here: if the Adriamycin chemo is the Red Devil, then this shot is the spawn of the Red Devil. The purpose of the Neulasta shot was to help combat the loss of my white blood cells. Chemotherapy would not only kill the cancer, but it would kill my healthy cells as well. By having the Neulasta shot, the hope was that my white blood count would not dip too low.

The shot hurt a bit, but I was not prepared for how it would make me feel later that night. My body ached like I had the flu. I felt feverish and cold at the same time. Add that to the nausea from the chemo and it equaled one unpleasant night. Again, I downed some meds and was off to bed early.

Thank goodness for Mark and my mom. They got the kids fed, bathed, and put to bed that night. Well, at least I think that's what happened. In my chemo/medicated-induced fog, I really was not sure what was going on beyond the discomfort that I was experiencing.

The next few days were up and down. I felt good one minute and cruddy the next. It was tricky to try and stay on top of my anti-nausea medication. I didn't want to take too many, but I didn't want to wait too long to take them either.

By Day 47, almost a week after chemo, I was in bad shape. To spare you the gruesome details, I will just say this--I pretty much had to camp out in the bathroom on Day 46. As a result, my body was sore and worn out. I could not get in a comfortable position. I had to cancel preschool for the day because I could not get out of bed. It was a horrible time for me.

By the time Mark got home from work that night, I could not even stand on my own two feet. I was sleep-deprived because of all the anxiety and the fact that I just could not get comfortable. I was at the end of my rope and asked him if he could give me a priesthood blessing.

That night, for the first time in weeks, I was able to sleep all the way until morning. If felt wonderful and I could add that miracle to the growing number of small miracles and tender mercies that had already been carrying me through my living nightmare.

> *Day 49: "I was seriously in so much pain. I could not get comfortable. I couldn't do anything. I just lay in bed all day. It was miserable and all I could do was think, 'I can't do this with every round. I can't!' But now, two days later, I remember that it was horrible, but since I am not experiencing that pain at this moment, I am not so worried about doing it again. Oh, I REALLY don't want to, but I made it through. I can do this. I can do these hard days because each day gets me one step closer to being finished. I have had a really hard time even looking at the pictures of my first chemo treatment. But I am slowly getting better. It was literally making me sick to my stomach to look at them or even think about going and having [chemo] again, [but today is a little bit better.]"*

The children and staff at Liberty Elementary School

At my first chemo treatment
September 2011

Fourteen: SAYING GOODBYE

Before I knew it, two weeks had flown by and it was time to go in for chemo round number two. I felt like I hadn't even been able to catch my breath from the first round and here it was, already time to go in for more torture. My hatred for cancer was growing.

For two weeks I had taken things one day at a time, sometimes one moment at a time. Fighting a newfound fatigue accompanied by bouts of nausea was a daily battle. I also spent most of my days trying to just be comfortable in my own skin, but not really succeeding because I could not pinpoint where my body was uncomfortable. I was just irritated all over.

I felt like I had aged about fifty years. It practically took a crane to get me out of bed or off the couch because my joints hurt so badly. My senses of smell and taste started to freak out. It felt like I was pregnant again, but the sensations were much more intense; like pregnancy on steroids.

I was still struggling to look at any of the pictures we had taken on the day of my first treatment. Seeing the bright red chemo sent shivers down my spine and just the thought of sitting in that chemo recliner again sent a wave of nausea rolling through my body.

~SAYING GOODBYE~

I woke up on Day 55, the day of my second treatment, and felt very unsure. I did not think my legs would be able to carry me through the cancer center's doors. I knew that I had to, but my brain and body were screaming, "No! We don't want to do that again!"

While contemplating all the ways I could possibly skip town, I started getting ready for the day. My hair had been dying a slow death and I was not looking forward to trying to make it look presentable. It would not hold curl anymore. The texture had changed making it impossible for me to do much of anything with it. As I ran my fingers through it, trying to decide what I should do, I gasped as a large section of hair came out in my hand.

I had known that this day would eventually come and I thought I had prepared myself for it. Unfortunately, I don't think any woman can really prepare herself for that moment of standing in front of the bathroom mirror, holding a chunk of precious hair in her hand.

As the tears started rolling down my cheeks, I let my thoughts wander to happier hair times. My hair and I have been through a lot together. I have had many hairstyles, some good and some very, very bad. Despite all the bad hair days (or 1992, which was my bad hair year), when it came right down to it, I really loved my hair!

I had tried using humor to cover up my true feelings of just how terrified I was to be bald. Some of my "hair-losing catch phrases" were:

"Yep! No more bad hair days for me!"

"Think of how much money I will save on hair products!"

"No more cleaning hair out of the sink or off the bathroom counters and floor."

"Think of how much time this will save me each morning!"

After all was said and done though, I was really going to miss my hair. I was not looking forward to losing it all. Sadly however, the time had come. I decided that my family and I would have a little going away party that night where we would take the clippers to my hair and say goodbye.

I pulled away from my thoughts and tried to make myself as presentable as possible. I wiped away the tears and resolved to face the day, no matter how hard it would be. After all, I had another chemo date with Mark and we had some cancer to kill.

My second round of chemo started off much differently than my first. For one thing, I knew exactly what was going to happen. There was no more mystery. Secondly, the photo opportunities had passed. I didn't even bring the camera or break out my phone.

I also could not look at the chemo as it was being administered. I couldn't even look at the nurse as he brought it in. I tolerated the ice chips, and knew that when it was time for round three, I would need to bring in something else to keep my mouth cold; something that I wouldn't end up hating. (Add my love of pellet ice to the growing list of things that cancer had robbed from me.)

After my treatment, I did everything I could to try and avoid nightfall and with it, my head-shaving party. I knew that once my hair was gone, the circle would be complete. I would look like a cancer patient and everyone would know that I was sick.

We gathered in the living room after dinner and plugged in the clippers. We had grand plans to do some crazy things with my hair in the process of shaving it--a Mohawk, old man hair, etc. However, my hair was just too limp to cooperate. It had fought a good fight and now it was ready to be done.

I had asked my kids to be part of this process. I felt that if they could participate in it, then maybe it would be less scary for them. They were each going to take a turn with the clippers. As they were discussing who would take the first turn, I felt my confidence waning. This was going to be much harder than I thought it would be.

68

To make matters worse, my little Ellie created some chaos in my heart. She came out of her room with her blanket covering her head. When I asked her to come out into the living room, she ran back into her bedroom and slammed the door shut. I could hear her soft little cries and it was too much for me to bear. I tried to go in and talk to her, but she would not let me in. She did not want to participate and there was nothing I could do about it.

My heart completely broke in that moment. I felt a surge of hatred for the cancer. It's one thing to make me cry and get upset. It's quite another to make one of my children cry. My "mama bear instinct" kicked in and I wanted to punch this thing called cancer right in the face.

I went back to my chair and tried to gain some composure while Mark talked to Ellie through her bedroom door. She was still not budging so we decided to go ahead without her. Why prolong the agony?

I heard the whir of the clippers as Josh flipped the switch. This was really happening. Josh gave the clippers to Emma because it was decided that she would go first. She stood next to me, and with tears streaming down her face, she took off a section of hair on the right side of my head. Our tears combined and silently fell to the floor with the soft wisps of hair. Abbie went next and took a section off the top. Then, it was Josh's turn. He did the left side of my hair, leaving only a few scraggly strands behind. I felt like I needed to take a turn as well, if only to feel like I had some sense of control over the situation.

One of my favorite photos from that night is of me running the clippers through my hair as Emma looked on. She was sobbing. I was trying to hold it

together. It depicts the emotions of the night perfectly.

In a matter of moments, the deed was done. My once beautiful hair was now in big clumps on the floor around me. I was now officially a cancer patient.

The girls and Josh each gathered a few pieces of my hair, some brown and some pink. Then I lovingly picked up the remaining pieces and threw them in the garbage.

As a mom, I have had so many moments where I have felt a rush of gratitude for the amazing kids that I have been blessed with. I experienced one of those moments while I was cleaning up the rest of my hair. My sweet son came up to me and said, "Mom, let's give me a buzz cut."

I had been teasing him for a few weeks, asking him if he would shave his head with me. He loved his longer, shaggy hair and would always laugh my suggestion off. However, the emotionally charged atmosphere of the night got the best of him. He could see how hard it had been for me to lose my hair and he wanted to do something to help. He sat down on the chair and in a few short minutes, Mark had given him a new hairdo.

Then it was my cute hubby's turn. Can I just pause here to tell you how much I love this wonderful man? I did not expect him to shave his head with me. He chose to do it because he loves me and wanted to support me in any way that he could. I started the process of shaving his head, but we ended up calling his mom to come over and finish the job so she could make it look neat and tidy.

The night had been extra hard, much harder than I ever imagined it would be. Only one thing made it tolerable and that was the support of my family. Not only my immediate family, but my extended family as well. I received a text from my dad the very next day. It was a picture of him with no hair. He wanted to pledge his support. He knew that the head shaving experience had been hard. Since he couldn't be with me the previous night, he offered his love in another way. He had walked into his barber's shop, told them he was there to support his daughter who was fighting cancer and came out with only stubble upon his head.

"I love this wonderful family of mine. With a shaved head, this cancer has certainly become real. But this family is who I am fighting for. They are my inspiration."

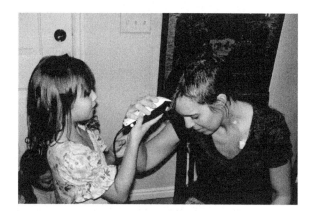

The next few days went by without too much of an incident. Ellie had come to accept my baldness and discovered that she really liked to rub my head. My preschool kids thought their teacher looked cool and some of them even brought me a new scarf to wear.

I started to think that I could actually be okay with the whole bald thing. Maybe it wasn't going to be such a big deal after all. I was pleasantly surprised at how nice and round my head was. There were no weird lumps or bumps. I thought that I looked pretty decent as a bald lady.

I relied mostly on hats as I was trying to figure out the best way to tie the scarves on my head. I had looked up a lot of tutorials on YouTube and must admit, that it was fun experimenting with different scarf styles.

~ONE DAY AT A TIME~

Three days had passed since our head-shaving party and I had mostly been home during that time. Only a few people had seen me with a hat or scarf, but only my immediate family had seen me completely bald. The real test of how the whole bald thing was going to work out for me was when Sunday rolled around and I needed to get ready for church.

Remember my catch phrase of, "Think of how much time I will save getting ready in the morning?" I was completely wrong. Learning to tie a headscarf was no easy task. On that particular Sunday morning, it was taking me just as long, if not longer, to get ready for church.

I couldn't make any of the styles look right. I tried on scarf after scarf with dress after dress until the mound of clothing on my bathroom floor was almost as tall as Ellie. I felt like a gypsy or a pirate. Not good looks for church, I'm afraid. Finally, I reached my breaking point, threw myself onto the pile of clothes, and cried my eyes out. This was at 8:45 in the morning. Our church began at 9 am and I was in charge of the Primary lesson that day.

"Well," I told myself, "this will not do."

I had a very important decision to make. I could either let the cancer win and stay home from church or I could suck it up and get on with my day. I chose the latter. I said a quick prayer, grabbed the scarf closest to me and tied the blasted thing on my head.

Mark had been following me around the house, wondering what he could say or do to make me feel better. I know he hated that I was feeling sad and he was wishing there was something he could do. So, he did the only thing he could do; he got the children in the car (along with the 25-lb. church bag that was overflowing with crayons, books, and treats to keep everyone occupied during Sacrament meeting), and waited for me to join them. Once I gained some control of my emotions, I got in the car and away we went, with smiles on our faces and tearstains on my cheeks.

We made it to church on time. I was able to make it through my lesson, through partaking of the Sacrament, and then I asked Mark to take me home. The nausea had kicked in and there was no way that I wanted to lose my cookies in the middle of church. I am sure that people would have understood, but there was no need to stick around and tempt fate.

On the way home, I felt empowered. I just did a really hard thing. Getting ready for church and then walking into the building were terribly difficult. I felt like I looked weird and different. But no one there cared. No one laughed or pointed. The primary kids didn't even bat an eye.

God sent angels to me that day. Earthly angels who made comments like, "I love that scarf! The coloring is so pretty with your skin tone", and "You look beautiful today!" Perhaps they were just being nice, but I didn't care. Those were words that were so helpful in giving me a much-needed boost of confidence.

I was so thankful that the first public place I had to go was to church, and to be among the people that I call my "ward family." I valued this great support system of people who loved me for who I was on the inside and not what I looked like on the outside. I also loved having a Savior who knew that I was feeling embarrassed and uncomfortable and who helped me be brave in those circumstances.

"I can do this. I can do hard things. I am trying to take this one step, one day at a time, and not let myself get overwhelmed."

Fifteen: DAY 65

"[I am] now on the upswing side of the cycle. [I have] been feeling pretty good the last couple of days-- still tired, but not as "yucky." It's really hard to describe the "yucky" feeling. [It's just a] bad combination of nausea, headaches, tiredness, and sometimes, body aches.

But once again I have to recognize God's hand in all of this. It could be so much worse. You hear horror stories about chemo and I [feel really] lucky to be getting off pretty easy. I know it's going to get worse before it gets better, but I also know that the Lord is carrying me through this. He has eased my burden immensely, and I know He will continue to do all that He can for me.

Brittany, and Chantelle, and my mom are doing a 5K walk/run for breast cancer today. I wish I could be there with them. It brings tears to my eyes, to think of the support system I have been blessed with. I have so many people who are loving me through this whole ordeal and it [continues] to amaze me every single day.

You know what else is fantastic about all [of] this? I love it when my preschoolers' parents or parents of former students have told me that their kids are praying for Ms. Desirae. And when I go to Primary and hear those

~DAY 65~

sweet kids [praying for me], I feel so lucky. The innocent prayer of a child is pure gold. There's nothing like it in the world.

I'm getting better at the whole scarf thing. It still feels a little weird to go out [with the scarf on my head.] I feel people [staring at me], but oh well. This is me and I am beautiful-- inside and out..."

Sixteen: TIME TO STRETCH AND GROW

As I begin this chapter, please allow me to backtrack a little. Approximately a week after my first chemo treatment, Mark received a phone call from our Stake Executive Secretary* who asked him if we could meet with the Stake President the following Sunday.

Generally, a meeting with the Stake President creates a stirring of anxiety among members of our church because most of the time, the President is not just calling you in to say hello. It means that there could possibly be some big changes in store for you.

Seeing as both of us already held stake callings**, we thought that maybe he wanted to meet with us so that he could release one or both of us from those responsibilities. We let that thought sit with us briefly, but the more we pondered it, the more we realized that the meeting was going to be something much bigger than that.

As we waited outside the President's office, my stomach began to churn. It was a combination of nausea from the chemo and nervousness for the conversation we were about to have. After welcoming us into his office, President Jess began the meeting with a few normal questions.

"How is everything going?" he asked. "Are your treatments going well and how are the kids handling everything?"

We answered that things were going well. I tried to be patient with the conversation, but I was hoping that we could move things along before my stomach got out of control. It was then that President Jess asked me an interesting question; one that I did not expect "Do you know why you are here today?"

"Yes, I...I think I do", I stammered. "You are going to extend the call to Mark to be Bishop of our ward, right?"

Indeed, that was what happened. Mark was called to be the Bishop of our ward. For those of you who are familiar with my church, you have some idea of what that calling entails. For those who are not familiar, a Bishop is the leader of a congregation with duties similar to that of a pastor or priest.

In other words, it would be a very demanding job in many aspects. There would be times where it could be very spiritually, emotionally, and physically draining. How in the world would we be able to tackle something like that while we were already investing so much of ourselves trying to win the battle with cancer?

As I mentioned earlier, Mark and I both had a feeling that this was coming. I don't say that to be prideful or sound as though we expected him to serve as Bishop someday. But rather, I know that the Holy Spirit prepared our Spirits. The Lord knew what our family was already going through. Because of this, He knew that our hearts would need to be prepped a little before we met with the Stake President.

In the days leading up to our appointment, a quote from Elder Richard G. Scott, an apostle of the Lord, came to my mind.

"Just when all seems to be going right, challenges often come in multiple doses applied simultaneously. When those trials are not consequences of your disobedience, they are evidence that the Lord feels you are prepared to grow

more. He therefore gives you experiences that stimulate growth, understanding, and compassion, which polish you for your everlasting benefit. To get you from where you are to where He wants you to be requires a lot of stretching, and that generally entails discomfort and pain."***

A little stretching and growing. I thought that fighting cancer would be enough stretching and growing for our little family. But the Lord felt that we could handle more.

I know that some people may have been wondering, "How can the Stake President ask that of their family right now? Doesn't he know that she has cancer and they have four young kids?" I can assure you that the Stake President was very aware of our family's situation. More importantly, as I mentioned, God knew of our family's situation.

The calling for Mark to serve as Bishop did not come from President Jess. It came from the Lord. The Stake President just extended that call to us. And although we felt a little trepidation, we were more than happy to accept the call to serve. Did that make us crazy? Probably. But it was a good crazy. It's a crazy that was totally dependent upon our faith in the Lord, Jesus Christ, and in His atoning sacrifice. We knew that we could do <u>anything</u> with the Lord by our side. The Lord knew that I would have cancer at the same time that He needed Mark to serve as Bishop. The key to surviving both of those challenges was this; we would not have to do either of them alone.

We left the Stake President's office feeling excited, nervous, and hugely overwhelmed. But we were ready to serve the people of our ward because we already had so much love for them.

When we arrived home, I called my parents so that I could share the news with them and my dad gave us some words of encouragement to ponder.

"Well. There is no better time for you to receive the blessings that come along with your husband serving as Bishop."

That was so true. If there was ever a time that I needed a blessing of strength that comes from serving the Lord, it was now. I had a family to raise, people to help, and a life to live. I would not be able to do those things without the Lord's help.

> *"Would the Lord really ask us to take on such a huge task right now? [Right along] with the little task of fighting cancer? I don't know what is in store for us, but I do know this...I will do whatever the Lord asks of us because He will not ask us to do more than we are able to. If He has faith in us, then I have faith in us too."*

Mark and I on the Sunday he was sustained as Bishop of our ward.

*A Stake Executive Secretary makes appointments for the Stake President. A Stake President is the man who presides over a stake, which is a group of wards.

**A calling is an opportunity to serve in our church. We believe that callings come because of revelation from God. We serve where God wants and needs us to be.

***Richard G. Scott, *"Trust in the Lord"*, LDS General Conference October 1995.

Seventeen: FIRST TO LAST

After the shock from our meeting with the Stake President had worn off a bit, I entered "battle mode" once again. By that point, I had somehow managed to survive three A/C chemo treatments, which left me with only one more to go.

My doctor had been right when he told me that each treatment would take me down a few more notches. Not only was I moving a bit slower, I was also feeling a lot more nauseated and "yucky".

"I have my last Red Devil treatment tomorrow. One hurdle [is] almost complete. But I think I may be hitting a wall here. I feel like I am slowly losing momentum and steam. I've been able to be strong through most of this process, but now I am tired. I told Mark the other day [that] I just want to sleep for the next six months. Sleeping is a great way to ignore your problems."

Day 84 brought my last A/C treatment. Good riddance. Sayonara. Ba-bye. As I prepared to say goodbye to this devil chemo, I thought about the differences between the first treatment and the last treatment.

With my first A/C treatment, my number one thought was, *"Yes! Finally! I can start doing something to kill this cancer!"* I had a tiny idea of what to expect, but no way of knowing exactly how the chemo would affect my body.

I was extremely anxious because of all the unknowns. When I saw the bright red chemo, it did not bother me, it intrigued me. I watched the entire administration process from start to finish. Mark took pictures of me, a smiling me, showing off my port, the chemo, and everything else. *"Look at me, everyone! I am having poison pumped into my body! Isn't it great?"* I felt like a champion afterwards, at least for a few days until the poison started ravaging my body.

By treatment number four, I was defeated. My spirit was deflated. There were no pictures. No smiling. No intrigue about the neon chemo, only loathing. In the days leading up to that last treatment, I had panic attacks just thinking about walking through the cancer center's doors.

The cancer center had a certain smell and although it was not a bad smell, it triggered horror in my mind. I could not get it out of my nostrils. The smell assaulted my nose the moment I opened the doors and I hated it.

I previously mentioned that after they administered the chemo, my port had to be flushed out with saline. That process left a strange, salty, and metallic taste at the back of my throat. It lingered there for hours after treatment and I loathed it.

As I braced myself to face A/C #4, I flip-flopped back and forth between two emotions--pure joy and devastating misery. I felt joyful because it would be my last "Red Devil" treatment and I would be free of its reign of terror. However, I was also in misery thinking about all that was in store for me once I made it home from the treatment.

When Day 84 finally arrived, I was very pensive. I just wanted to get it over with quickly. Again, I could not look at the chemo, or any part of the process. My limp body sagged in the chemo recliner. The only time I spoke was when someone asked me a question. I could not wait to get out of there, get to my house, and crawl into my bed.

With the previous treatments, I could usually plan on the side effects waiting to kick in for at least a day, sometimes two. That was not the case with the last treatment. As I dragged myself to bed, I felt like I had been run over by a truck--a very big truck.

I downed my nausea pills like they were Cadbury Mini eggs (mmm...Cadbury Mini Eggs), even though they had pumped me full of anti-nausea meds before administering the chemo. I had finally reached the point where the thought of throwing up sounded nice.

"Maybe if I throw up I will actually feel better!", I thought to myself.

That night was horrid. After tossing and turning for over an hour, I was finally able to find a position (lying on my stomach with my face buried in my pillow) that allowed me to quell the nausea. *"Please, oh please just let me throw up!"* I thought. *"If I could just throw up once, maybe that familiar and dreaded ache in my belly will leave!"*

Sadly, I did not throw up. I just lay there and willed myself to think of something else--anything else: a beautiful sandy beach, the warm summer sun, or Disneyland with my kids. Those images swam around in my brain as I finally drifted off to sleep.

It was a fitful night as I had to wake up a few times to take more nausea pills. I woke up the next morning feeling as though I had never gone to sleep in the first place. My goal for the day was to just make it through preschool. After that and the little excursion of getting my Neulasta shot, I planned to fumble my way back into my bed and stay there for the rest of the afternoon.

The following day (a Friday) I lounged around most of the morning. By afternoon, I was able to drag myself out of the house to go to the grocery store with Mark. I barely made it through that experience.

My feet felt like they were filled with lead, making it impossible to move any faster than a snail. The nerves in my back were highly sensitive to touch and even the simple act of wearing a shirt created intense pain. Since I couldn't run around topless, I just had to grit my teeth and bear the searing pain.

By the time Saturday rolled around, my back nerves had calmed down a bit, but my energy level was still hanging right around the zero mark. Because of my lack of energy, I started to wonder if my doctor would recommend a blood transfusion. That thought created fear and frustration. I was fearful only because I had never had a transfusion and the unknown aspects of that were scary. The frustration came because if I did need a transfusion, it would just be one more thing to add to my already full plate.

> *"I am ready for the 'Get Out of Jail Free' card now. The past few days have not been good. The last treatment has hit me like a ton of bricks and I am down and out for the count...I am in the 'I give up' mode. I am trying hard not to be, but I have reached the end of one rope and I am wondering where to find the next one to grab on to. I know there are still so many prayers being said on my behalf and I am trying to cling to them as much as I can. But I am hitting a brick wall and it's going to take some time to work my way over the top."*

The feelings of self-pity and depression hung thick in the air. As much as I tried to feel happy that my "Red Devil" treatments were done, I just couldn't muster any joy. I could not stop myself from thinking about the next four rounds of chemo and the side effects that it would bring.

I was already experiencing so many unpleasant side effects that it was hard to imagine going through any more. The nausea, fatigue, and achiness were a constant presence. Then there was the hair loss, of course, and it was cold walking around without any hair! Plus, the nerves in my head were almost as agitated as the nerves in my back. That made wearing a scarf or hat or anything else a painful experience.

Fortunately, I had not lost my eyebrows or eyelashes yet. The bald issue I was dealing with, but I was really worried about losing those precious features. Well, maybe the eyebrows would not be such a big deal. I could always pencil those on and maybe I could even have some fun with it. As in, "Uh oh, Mommy has her angry eyebrows on today! Watch out!"

However, the eyelashes presented a bigger problem. I would not be able to wear fake eyelashes because of the risk of infection. The thought of walking around without any eyelashes really freaked me out. I could just picture myself-- bald, hunched over from pain, and no eyebrows or eyelashes. It would not be a good look for me.

Aside from still having to deal with those side effects, the new chemo would bring with it a host of other goodies such as losing finger and toenails, added muscles aches, possibly more nausea and fatigue, and neuropathy (numbness and pain from nerve damage). How could I possibly deal with more? I imagined that by the time I was through with all the chemo, I was going to be a big puddle of Des on the floor.

With all the side effects I was dealing with, the one that bothered me the most was not anything physical. Rather, it was seeing the pain and worry in my kids' faces. It was watching them come to my bedside with tears in their eyes. I will never be able to erase those images from my mind.

This creature writhing about in pain was not their mommy. Their mom always helped them with homework, activities, practicing, and finding the perfect after-school snack. Now she was in bed most of the afternoon, or shuffling around the house, barely able to move.

I hated seeing the pain and sorrow in their eyes knowing that there was nothing I could do to fix it. My hope was that time would heal all wounds and that they would not be too scarred, emotionally, from this ordeal.

"Well, 90 days [have gone by]. How do I feel 90 days into this cancer journey? Exhausted--physically, emotionally, spiritually, you name it. I am all tapped out. (Mmm, that makes me think of root beer and that sounds really good right about now...weird.)

The past few days have been really low for me. I haven't felt like doing much and so, I haven't done much. I've done preschool and tried to do some 'mom things', but mostly I have just sat or slept. I hate that. It is so foreign to me.

When I began this process, I was thinking that I could still continue my 'year of crafting' like I had planned. But the thought of getting everything out and then having to clean it up again does not sound like fun.

I really would take two more years as PTA president over this whole cancer biz. Hands down. No contest and <u>that</u> was hard work. [Tomorrow] I go in for another PET scan. Do you want to know what my dream is? It's a big one. One I just might need a fairy godmother for. Here it is...

I dream that the PET scan will show no [signs of] cancer. My doctor will call me and say, 'Guess what? I think we can skip the next round of chemo and just go straight to surgery and radiation.' Wouldn't that be lovely? [There have been] miracles all along this journey and I would love to count that as another miracle, but I think it's probably just going to stay a dream. I had to go in for some blood work today and while I was waiting to talk to the doctor, I heard someone ring the chemo bell. (There is a bell in the chemo room that you get to ring after your last treatment is completed.) It took all I could do not to cry. I want to ring that bell so badly!"

Eighteen: MR. TAXOTERE

My dream about the PET scan showing no traces of cancer <u>did</u> come true. However, there was no phone call from my doctor suggesting that we skip the next round of chemo. While I was not looking forward to another four rounds of sitting in that chemo recliner, the medication seemed to be working, which meant that I needed to stick with the plan.

My first dose of Taxotere was on Day 104. Everything went well which was a blessing. Receiving that chemo was not as scary as the A/C chemo because no one needed to put a HAZMAT suit on or anything like that. The medication came in a simple IV bag and if I didn't know any better, I would have thought it was saline.

The chemo only took an hour to administer, so I felt like we were in and out of there, which was also a nice change of pace. Surprisingly, I felt pretty good for the rest of that day and the next. Say, maybe "Mr. Taxotere" wasn't as bad as I thought he would be! Sadly, I was wrong.

Two days after my treatment, I decided that since I had been feeling good, I would try and catch up on a few things (and by a few things, I mean A LOT of things.) I began by decorating our Christmas tree. I did have two of my friends there helping me, so the task was not as laborious as it could have been, but I probably did more than I should have.

After the tree was completed and beautiful, I drove to the mall to attempt some Christmas shopping. Then I baked some cookies, took the girls to the ice rink for some skating time, and ended the day by attending a Christmas party at the church. That is a busy day for someone whose body is functioning at normal capacity. My body was only capable of functioning at minimal capacity and about halfway through the Christmas party, it began to shut down.

I found Mark and told him that we needed to get home as quickly as possible. We rounded up the kids and drove the short distance to our home. As soon as we arrived, I collapsed on my bed and that is where I stayed all night and through the next day. I had definitely over-stepped my bounds and my body was letting me know it.

In combination with the chemo and Neulasta shot side effects, I had come down with a cold or flu virus as well. My joints screamed every time I tried to move. I could not get out of bed without every muscle yelling in protest.

I called Dr. Chandramouli's office and they told me to start taking my back-up antibiotics. They had been sitting in my medicine basket since the first round of chemo, just waiting for a moment such as this. I yanked the lid off and swallowed that first pill as fast as I could then went back to bed and settled in for a very miserable weekend.

By Monday I was starting to feel more like myself, which was a good thing because my baby was turning five. My family had already sacrificed so much, and I had to draw the line at letting cancer ruin someone's birthday. That would not be acceptable.

My mother-in-law came over that morning to help with a few chores and then she whisked me and Ellie off to the magical land of Target. We slowly roamed the aisles of toys until Ellie had found the perfect present. We grabbed some lunch and then grandma took us home and left me alone with the birthday girl. We spent the afternoon cuddling on the couch and watching movies. Although it wasn't the most exciting of birthday celebrations, under the circumstances, it was absolutely perfect.

A week went by and I was still feeling a little under the weather. Because of the virus and the fact that I had lost my nose hairs, my nose had become a leaky faucet. (Did you know that chemo causes your nose hairs to fall out?) I had never realized just how important those little nose hairs were until I didn't have them anymore. I carried a box of lotion-infused tissues with me wherever I went. I hope whomever invented those "tissues from heaven" gets some extra good karma. They made a world of difference for my sore, red nose.

In between chemo treatments, I had to go in and have my blood levels checked to make sure that my red and white blood cell counts didn't dip too low. Because I was still feeling sick and my fatigue had worsened, I was a little nervous for this round of blood testing.

After my last round of the A/C chemo, I barely escaped being sent to the hospital for a blood transfusion. Although I had heard that blood transfusions were not really anything to be nervous about, I was feeling a little scared. It was also just one more thing for me to have to do; one more bump in a road already filled with so many potholes.

When the doctor came into the room to share the results of my blood check, I braced myself for the bad news.

"Your blood levels are really, really low this week," she said. "Normal red cell count should be between 37-48. Yours is 25 and you are dehydrated. I am strongly recommending that you go in for a blood transfusion tomorrow."

Wow. Twenty-five? No wonder I felt so sluggish. I was only running on about half of the red blood cells that I needed for my body to function. (Sigh.) Okay. I suppose having a blood transfusion was a must.

That night was one of the most memorable nights of my journey. Because Mark was serving as the Bishop of our ward, he had appointments 2-3 nights of the week. This unforgettable night happened to be one of the nights that he needed to be away from home for a few hours. Normally I didn't mind him being gone. Our kids were usually pretty helpful and it was nice to just sit in a quiet house for a bit once they had been sent to bed.

With that said, this night was not your typical "Dad is gone to meetings" night. I could tell that Mark was very concerned about the state that I was in. He repeatedly asked if he should cancel his appointments so that he could stay home and help me with the nightly routine.

"Yes!" my insides were screaming. *"I need you to be with me!"* Unfortunately, I decided to be a martyr and my insides did not win.

"No, it's ok. Just go," I said. "Josh and Emma can help me. We will be fine."

I could tell that he did not want to leave me, but I was insistent that he not cancel his meetings. He reluctantly grabbed his keys, gave me a kiss, and headed out the door.

As the garage door was closing, I realized that I had made a huge mistake. It was time to begin the bedtime routine, which was no easy task. It consisted of me asking everyone at least five times to pick up their stuff that was placed in piles all over the house. Then there was the gentle persuading (more like impatient nagging) to get PJ's on and teeth brushed. Finally, I had all the kids gathered into one room so that we could read stories, scriptures, and say a prayer.

I made it through one story and a few verses of scripture before the natives got restless and started pelting me with the usual stalling tactics.

"I need a drink!"

"I'm hungry."

"Ellie's blanket is touching my bed!"

"I'm not tired!"

To which I replied, "You just had a drink and a bedtime snack."

"Just move Ellie's blanket."

"I don't care if you are not tired, it's bedtime."

And of course, there was my usual, "Josh, do not put your sister in a headlock."

~ONE DAY AT A TIME~

I decided that story time was over and tried to stand up. As I attempted that simple task, my legs buckled and would not support my weight. I crashed to the floor and sat there, a bit stunned by what had just happened.

When I first started chemo and was being informed about all the side effects, I had a hard time imagining what it would be like to not have any energy. Surely, I would always be able to do simple tasks like walking or doing a load of laundry!

Well, now there was nothing left to the imagination. I had reached that point. I could not stand up. My joints ached too badly and my legs were so weak that they could not support my weight.

The tears started flowing, freely and quickly until I was sobbing. I lay there on the floor, feeling very much defeated. The room was silent except for the sounds of me gasping for breath as the sobs wracked my body. My kids surrounded me and tried to help me stand, but I just couldn't do it. Then they all started crying because it was a scary situation for them and they felt totally helpless.

I knew that I had to gain some control over the situation so that I could calm their fears. I pulled myself up into a kneeling position and said, "It's alright guys. I'm okay. I'm just really, really tired and I can't stand up right now. Everything will be fine. It's just because my blood count is low. But I am going to get that fixed tomorrow and then my body will feel better."

I can't remember which one of us suggested that we say a prayer, but that's exactly what we did. I felt an immediate wave of peace touch my heart. The kids were calm as well and it was a wonderful experience for all of us.

Everyone sprang into action. There was no more arguing, no more stalling. Just hugs and kisses, and "I love you's." I literally crawled to my bedroom and Josh helped me get up into my bed. He gave me a hug and a kiss, made sure that I didn't need anything else and then headed down to his own room.

I lay there in my bed just looking up at the ceiling and thought, "*How did I get here? I can't do this anymore! I can't even stand up! How am I ever going to make it through this?*" The tears started flowing again. It was most definitely a low moment for me.

90

~MR. TAXOTERE~

"I am just tired of it all. Tired of having my kids have to make sacrifices and miss out on fun things. Tired of trying to force myself to eat when I can't taste [anything] and I feel full after two bites. [I am] tired of going in for chemo. I really want to call and say, 'I'm done. [I] can't do it anymore.' But I am going to continue to fight even though I feel like there's not much fight left in me. I am battered and bruised, but keep stumbling to my feet. I will beat this cancer. I will be here to raise my kids for years to come.

I will be here to help others through their battles and trials. My Savior will help me do this. I can't do it without Him. He carries me through the rough patches, and helps me struggle to my feet after each knockdown."

Nineteen:

RENEWED ENERGY

On Day 117, I checked into the hospital for my blood transfusion and I was surprised to be assigned to an actual room. I was expecting to be in a room full of recliners like the chemo room that I was accustomed to. Instead, I got my own bed, scratchy sheets and all. Okay, so it wasn't the Ritz Carlton, but it was better than a slippery, cold, vinyl recliner.

I said a silent prayer of thanks for this heart-warming surprise. It's funny how something as trivial as having your own room to be in while you have someone's blood pumped through your veins can bring such joy to your life.

After I got settled on the bed, the nurse attempted to access my port. The poor thing; I think it was the first port she had ever seen. I was beginning to wonder if she had actually attended nursing school. I had to guide her, step by step because by now, I was an expert on accessing a port (even though *I* had never attended nursing school.) I suppose I considered myself an expert by experience.

At one point, I really wanted to tenderly take everything out of her shaky, unstable hands and do it myself. It probably would have been faster and a lot less nerve-wracking for the both of us.

She finally called someone to help her and fortunately, that person knew exactly what to do. With my port finally ready to roll, there was only one more thing to do before I welcomed someone else's blood into my body.

My doctor had sent in an order for my blood to be tested to see if it was harboring any sort of bacterial infections. I had been running a low-grade fever for a few weeks, along with the cold and sinus issues. He just wanted to cover all the bases, which I appreciated.

However, I did not realize how much blood the nurses would need to take for this seemingly simple test. Seriously! That blood was a precious commodity and I wasn't sure that I wanted to give that much of it away! They filled up two small soda style bottles, enough blood to satisfy at least ten thirsty vampires. I braced myself to be lightheaded, but fortunately, that feeling never came.

Finally, it was time to hook me up to the good stuff. As I watched the thick, Jell-O like liquid slowly flow through my port, I felt my body cheer. It was tired of being tired and I hoped that this blood would give me the boost I needed to move forward.

I also thought about how grateful I was that someone had so unselfishly taken time out of his or her busy schedule to go to the Red Cross and donate this blood. I have donated blood once in my life and almost passed out afterwards. Now, because of the poison that had coursed through my veins, I would not be able to donate blood for a long time. I would not be able to pay it forward in that way for a few years. I offer a big thank you to all those who can and do take the time to donate blood. It really does save lives in more ways than one.

I was required to receive two units of blood. Each unit took approximately two hours to administer. I slept through most of the first one because they had given me some Benadryl to combat any allergic reaction that might occur. But I was mostly coherent through the second unit and decided that it was nice to have a few quiet hours to be with the Love of my Life.

I was so thankful to have Mark by my side during that difficult time. I hated that I had to be a burden to him, although he never made me feel like a burden. He was so good about making me feel loved and supported and I will never be able to thank him enough for loving me through my battle.

It was also in the quiet moments of that day, as I watched the steady drip of a stranger's blood, that I had a realization. I finally felt like I was able to put into words exactly what I felt like: A Bop Bag. Do you know what that is? It is an oblong-shaped, plastic punching bag that stands about four feet tall. Usually it has a character's face and body plastered on it, like Superman or Bozo the Clown. The purpose of a bop bag is to be able to punch it over and over again and after every punch, the bop bag has no choice but to pop back up. It can do this because the base of it is filled with sand, which keeps it stable.

That was me; a giant Des Bop Bag. Trial after trial, challenge after challenge; I kept getting punched in the face, with no other choice but to stand upright and get punched again. Like the bop bag, I had a stable, sand-filled base. My base consisted of my family, friends, and my belief in my Savior, Jesus Christ. Those are the three things that helped me rise up and take the next punch. They helped me stand when I didn't have the strength to stand on my own. As long as I had them in my corner, I knew that I would be able to continue to take the punches, no matter how hard they became.

Twenty:

MY CHRISTMAS WISH

My second Taxotere treatment came just a few days before Christmas, which was Day 125 on my journey. That was on a Wednesday and by Friday of that week, my whole body ached from head to toe. I kept my pain medication handy and tried to get some last-minute Christmas things done.

I had only one wish for Christmas, and that was that there would be enough Tylenol and Ibuprofen in the world to keep the nasty body aches at bay. I wanted to enjoy the glorious Christmas weekend with my family, free from the debilitating aches and pains. I could not stay in bed the whole weekend like I did with the first Taxotere treatment, not with kids who were bursting with excitement every minute of every day.

Christmas was coming! I loved Christmas and all the wonderful family traditions that came with it. There was absolutely <u>no</u> way that I was going to let cancer get in the way of keeping those traditions and having a magical Christmas.

One of our traditions is going to the zoo on Christmas Eve day. I was determined not to skip this tradition, even if it meant that I had to be pushed around in a wheelchair; which is exactly what happened.

Unfortunately, what we rented from the zoo could hardly be classified as a wheelchair. It was more like a "death trap on wheels." I remember thinking, *"Great. I have been on the road to you know where, fighting for my life every inch of the way, and now I am going to die in this rickety, rented wheelchair".*

The kids were more than happy to take turns pushing me. They were excited for Christmas, the zoo, and to push their sickly mother in a wheelchair. It's the little things that bring us excitement, right? I tried to be patient as they did their best to push me with care, but I found myself cringing with every turn and I became an expert at blocking myself from hitting fences, buildings, and people.

I received a lot of "watch where you are going" looks which were immediately followed by the "oh, I'm sorry you're sick" looks. I was used to having people stare or give sympathetic looks because of the whole bald thing, but combine that with riding around in a wheelchair and you suddenly become the center of attention.

None of the looks really bothered me because we were at the zoo fulfilling our Christmas tradition. Although it was a bit of a harrowing experience, I survived it, rickety wheelchair and all. My heart was filled with gratitude.

Later that afternoon we spent time with the Ogden family, but truth be told, the only thing I remember is being swallowed up in my father-in-law's comfy blue recliner, watching the action ensue around me. It was a glorious way to spend the afternoon.

"We made it home about 7:30 pm and finished reading 'The Best Christmas Pageant Ever.' We love that book. We had a nice discussion with the kids when we finished reading it. We talked to them about how the light of Christ works in people. I can't tell you how many times in the last few months that I have had people tell me that I am glowing, that my beauty is shining through. I appreciate comments like this because that tells me that I am doing something right. The light that is shining through me is the light of my Savior.

When [people] make those comments, it opens up an opportunity for me to share my testimony with them...

My energy levels are slowing sinking lower and lower. I am not sure when they are going to be back to 'normal' or whatever my post-chemo normal will be. [However], I know that my Savior continues to carry me through the rough patches. He walks by my side, supporting me on those days when I can almost make it.

People keep telling me how brave I am. I don't really feel extra brave or [braver] than anyone else. I am [only] doing what I have to do to take care of my family and [to] do what God needs me to do. I really don't see any other choice. Giving up is not an option, so forging ahead is what I am going to do."

That Christmas I received my one wish. God blessed me to be able to enjoy the holiday season with my family. He did not take the body aches and pains away, but He did strengthen me to be able to endure them. It turned out to be one of the most magical Christmas seasons of my life and I owe that all to God and my family.

Twenty-One:

HAPPY NEW YEAR

I am ready for a few things...

1. I am ready for my hair again. I want to wash it, blow dry it, style it, braid it, pull it up in a ponytail, curl it, straighten it, you name it. I want it back.

2. I am ready to have my normal sense of taste [back]. I can't describe how weird my taste is, but I am ready for the weirdness to be gone.

3. I am ready to not talk about cancer anymore. Almost every-where I go it's always the same thing. 'How are you doing?' 'Only two treatments left, hooray!' 'Hang in there!' 'You look beautiful!' All of those comments are wonderful and I am so appreciative of everyone's love and concern, but I DON'T WANT TO TALK ABOUT CANCER ANYMORE!!

4. I am ready to have my energy back. I hate having to plan my days with time for a rest after every little thing I do. Clean up

a room--REST--[teach] preschool--REST--Fix a meal--REST--Run an errand or two--REST, etc.
I am just ready to be me again, but I know it's never going to be quite the same."

The beginning of the new year brought with it a lot of grumpiness and only a little bit of joy, unfortunately. I was so completely ready to be done with chemo, cancer, and everything else that it was causing a major amount of crabbiness.

I was delighted and thankful, of course, to be celebrating a new year when just a few months prior, I was unsure if I would be around to celebrate any more new years. I always had that piece of gratitude in the back of my mind. But it was very hard to celebrate and be happy when I just felt awful.

As I have mentioned before, going through chemotherapy has standard side effects, but those side effects vary from person to person, and I think that most cancer patients have a hard time coming up with words that accurately describe how chemo makes you feel. There are only two words that I have been able to come up with..."blah" and anger.

One of the things that was really bothering me was my loss of taste. I am a foodie and I love to eat. Because of the chemo, things that once tasted delicious, now gagged me. I had never been one for spicy foods, but now I found that I could hardly eat anything that had more than a few specks of black pepper. If there was more than that, my tongue felt like it was on fire. However, the most terrible part of this taste conundrum was that anything sweet tasted like cardboard. It sucked all the joy right out of chocolate, one of my favorite pre-cancer treats.

As if to add further insult to injury, my sense of smell was not affected much. I could smell all the tantalizing aromas of my favorite foods, but the moment I put them into my salivating mouth, I wanted to spit them right back out. That made me really grumpy when mealtimes rolled around.

Dinnertime used to be such a great time for our family. We would laugh about our days and enjoy spending the time together. Suddenly there was a black cloud hovering over the dinner table because my grumpiness permeated the air. Dinnertime just meant that I had to force feed myself and think about how wonderful food used to taste. I couldn't focus on having a conversation with my family because I was too determined to be cantankerous about my ailing taste buds.

Another thing that was really eating away at me was my baldness. I really missed my hair. It had been fun to try out different knots and styles with the scarves. I had even learned how to accessorize them with flower clips, but the "funness" had now worn off. (Pretty sure I made up a new word there, but it fits.)

My list of positive things about losing one's hair did not seem so positive anymore. I just wanted my hair back. It was trying, bless its little heart. I had a thin layer of what I would call "peach fuzz." It was so tiny, fine, and wispy that I couldn't even take a picture of it, but it was there, and it brought a tiny dose of excitement to my pity party.

I considered myself a pretty positive person, and usually could pick out the bright side of every situation. However, it seemed like at that time in my journey, it was getting harder and harder to stay positive. I was still good at putting on my game face. I didn't think that it was necessary to make everyone else miserable just because I was. Unfortunately, there were days that the game face just would not show up and those were the days that I tried to stay home in bed.

It was a very depressing time for me. It was the middle of winter and I felt like the season correlated closely to my place in this journey. I was experiencing the "winter" portion of cancer, the time when everything felt dark and dreary. It was hard for me to remember what it felt like to be warm and bask in the sun's illustrious rays. I knew that spring was just around the corner, but that didn't help much when the blizzard was raging.

I felt very abandoned. I experienced days when even though I knew better, I felt like God had forgotten how miserable I was and that I needed help. I tried to be positive and count my blessings, but the darkness was too overwhelming.

"Almost 150 days [of] living with cancer. Some days it still feels so surreal. Other days I just have to stop and look in the mirror and I am instantly

reminded that this is for real. [I have] seven chemo treatments down. Only one more to go. The time has gone by slowly and quickly at the same time. Each day seems to go by slowly, but when I look back on the whole experience, I can't believe that it has been 148 days.
I am almost a puddle on the floor. With each chemo treatment, I lose a bit more stamina. I will be so happy when this portion of the journey is over. I know that there are still going to be hard times ahead, but if I can just get this poison crap over, that would be wonderful."

"Day 161: [It was not a great] night for me. I was too concerned with doing unimportant things on the computer, which made me ornery and impatient with [my kids] ... I have been granted a second chance with them.
But instead of being with them, I sit at the computer. Grr. We all had major tantrums tonight. It was not a pretty sight. *Sigh* Tomorrow is a new day though. I am ready to commit again. Even though I live in a constant state of 'yuckiness', I am ready to be a better mom. To not act irritated when they ask me to do something or help them or listen to them. I've got to be better and stay better.
The only way I am going to be able to do that is to stay close to my Savior. I've got to study the scriptures--no--devour them. Satan knows my weaknesses and he is having a good time playing on them right now. Well, I say, no more. Change is in the air."

The new year had not started off very well. Amid the swirling winds of depression and sorrow, I had a hard time finding my footing. But I was not giving up. My time with chemo was drawing to a close. I just had to find the strength to keep moving forward.

Twenty-Two:

CHEMO BE GONE!

It finally came, the day of my last chemo treatment. When I started my chemo journey in the fall, February 1st seemed like it was a million miles away. There were days when I thought that I would never make it to the finish line. But just like everything else in life, there is a beginning and an ending, and this adventure was finally coming to an end.

Mark and I had decided that this was an occasion worthy of checking the kids out of school for the day. Mama was only planning on ringing that chemo bell once ya know. The excitement flowing through our home that morning was palpable. Day 167 was going to be a great day.

As we drove to the cancer center, I was a giant, jittery ball of nerves and exhilaration. Unfortunately, I got a lap full of root beer because of it. Right as we were pulling into the parking lot, my cup slipped and the bubbly brown liquid drenched my new shirt and the passenger seat in Mark's car.

As I watched the delicate, pink lace trim get soaked with the brown fluid, I felt the tears forming. That was not how I wanted to begin this beautiful day!

Then, just like that, I snapped out of it. There was no time for crying over spilled root beer; I had a chemo journey to finish.

I went through the usual check in procedures and then the moment arrived. I planted myself in that chemo recliner for the very last time. It was the last time that I would have that awful metallic taste in my mouth as they flushed my port to get it ready for the chemo. The last time I would have to watch the endless drip, drip, drip of the poison going into my veins. It would also be the last time that I would have to "look forward" to the evil Neulasta shot and all the thrilling side effects that came along with it.

"I was feeling very antsy and couldn't make the time go by fast enough. But finally, the last drop had fallen and I was done. D-O-N-E! Time to ring the bell, baby! After [the nurse] unhooked me [from all of the IV tubes, the kids and I] grabbed our stuff and headed over to the bell. My girls and I took hold of the rope that I had been waiting so long to touch. I had walked by that bell many times, looking at it longingly and now, my time had come."

As I felt that scratchy rope in my hand, a jolt of rapture ran through me. It was time. Only a few weeks before that day I had watched as someone else grabbed onto that rope and rang it like his life depended on it. As I had watched that person, I felt a strange mixture of love and hate race through my heart. I felt love, because I was so happy that he had reached that milestone in his journey and I felt hate, because I so desperately wanted that to be me.

I am sure that as I was ringing the bell, someone else was experiencing his or her own love/hate feelings. But I couldn't be bothered with thoughts of anyone else at that moment. As I rang that bell, I was in a moment of pure selfishness and joy.

And it was a perfect moment until the heavy brass bell came crashing down on my little Abbie Kadabbie's hand. Not cool, chemo bell! Not cool! Fortunately, Abbie was not hurt and now that experience just makes the day that much more memorable for us. I suppose that we were on such a super adrenaline high that we didn't realize our own strength.

After gently putting the bell back on the wall, we took our troop of supporters and headed home. Now that the bell-ringing portion of this day was over, it was time to go home and participate in the dream come true that was waiting there for me.

About 17 days before my last chemo treatment, I had written a blog post in which I had described a party that would be the perfect ending to the chemo chapter of my journey. For the party, I envisioned a ton of family and friends, pink balloons and streamers, pink cupcakes and drinks, a lot of laughing and hugging, and maybe even some shedding of happy tears.

As I pondered the sublime party, I figured that it would only stay in my head because there was no way I was going to have the strength or energy to plan it. I got exhausted just thinking about it, and unfortunately, party planning was not one of Mark's strong suits.

Enter my friend, Jenn. Almost as soon as I had clicked "publish" for the blog post, she responded with an email that basically said, "You want a party? I've got that covered for you. Consider it a done deal." And she did not mess around either. The party ended up being everything I had imagined and more. But I am getting ahead of myself here. Let's go back to the drive home...

"Pulling onto our street was surreal. There were pink balloons on every light pole. When I actually saw the house, I could not believe [my eyes.] My yard was filled with pink balloons, [as was] my porch. There was a 'Happy No More Chemo Day' sign hanging [by the door] and cars lining the driveway. We finally made it inside [the house] and I looked around at all of the wonderful people there. Most of them had come early to help decorate and everything looked amazing.

There was one face [in the crowd] that I was totally shocked to see there. It was Melissa, my best friend from high school. She had driven all the way from Southern Utah. She was only able to stay for the party and then would have to drive back home. Well, I immediately started crying. I could not believe it."

From the moment I hugged Melissa until about 9 pm that night, it was non-stop partying. I felt so alive! It seemed as though my house had a revolving door and I could not believe that all those people would take a few moments out of their busy lives to stop by and celebrate with me. My home was filled with treats, laughter, hugging, tears, and it looked like it had been bathed in Pepto-Bismol. It was absolutely perfect and I couldn't have imagined a better way to say goodbye to chemo.

I fell into my bed that night, exhausted as I came down from the adrenaline charged high I had been on. As I lay there with thoughts of the party swimming around in my head, I closed my eyes and congratulated myself.

"You did it," I thought. And then I drifted off to sleep with a smile on my face and the knowledge that chemo was finally gone from my life.

Me and Melissa

My decorated front porch

Twenty-Three: BRING IT ON

Now that chemo was over, I started to look ahead to the next pit stop on my race to beat cancer: my bilateral mastectomy. There were 28 days between my last chemo treatment and that surgery. I spent those days focused on coping with the lasting side effects from the chemo.

I think people often assume that once someone has completed all his/her rounds of chemo then he/she is done, finished, back to normal. Oh, if only that were true. I had side effects that lasted for years after I had finished with the chemo treatments. They definitely lessened over time, but they were still there.

As I waited for the day of my surgery to arrive, I spent most of the time being completely exhausted. Each day, it took all the strength I could muster to just make it out of bed. My joints ached and my muscles were fatigued. I was also still dealing with bouts of nausea. My hair was slowly trickling in, but I was losing my fingernails and toenails at an alarming rate. The poor things looked as though a hammer had pummeled them. They were black and blue and so tender to the touch!

I am also sad to say that my eyebrows and eyelashes finally succumbed to the poison. They hung on as long as they could, the poor things. That was probably because, according to my husband, I had the world's toughest eyebrows. He was always teasing me about how wiry they were. But I will take wiry eyebrows if it meant that they could hang on clear until the end of my chemo treatments. I even had a few who must have been like Navy Seals or something because they never left me. Bless you, you sweet little eyebrow soldiers. By staying, you made me feel and look less like an alien.

In the day or two before my surgery, my good friends, Panic and Anxiety, decided to pay a visit. They had been hovering near the doorway for a little while, waiting for me to get comfortable. Now they saw an opportunity to fill my mind with worry, sorrow, and fear, and they took it.

I would be performing a simple task such as, loading the dishwasher, when the reality of the surgery slapped me across the face. I was in my early 30's and would be losing my breasts soon. Really, how did this all happen? The tears would begin to trickle down my cheeks and the sadness forced me to stop whatever task I was doing.

After each tear fest, I would remind myself of how fortunate I was to be to this point in the journey and be facing such a hopeful and positive outcome. My latest PET scan showed no presence of cancer anywhere and my doctors were all positive that once the mastectomy was complete, there would be no trace of the cancer left behind.

As I dried my tears and returned to my task, the sadness lingered a bit. I was sad to be losing this part of me, but I was ready to say goodbye to the "girls." Although they were a part of me for many years, I disliked them the moment I found out they were trying to kill me. They had to go.

Finally, the day of my surgery arrived. Mark and I stepped out of the car and into the chilly early hours of the morning. We walked into the hospital, hand in hand, feeling calm and as ready as we were going to be.

Panic and Anxiety had been forced to pack their bags and I was filled with a perfect feeling of sweet stillness. I had angels in my corner, both here and in heaven. I also had the assurance that God loved me and would take care of me. I felt that everything would be fine.

After I checked in and we were situated in a room, I had to get dressed in a terribly stiff hospital gown. It was not like the other gowns that I had been offered before. At least those ones were somewhat soft and flowy. This was one stiff and scratchy. It was not comfortable and I was just about ready to say, "Thanks, but no thanks", when the nurse showed me the gown's magical powers.

She drew my attention to a grommet near the top of the gown. In that grommet, she placed one end of a long hose. The other end was connected to a small machine on the wall behind me. Finally, she flipped a switch and in an instant I was enveloped in warmth that spread from my shoulders to my toes. Just a few moments earlier I was cursing whoever had invented this uncomfortable gown and now, I was blessing them. It was a feeling of pure bliss and I settled down into the hospital bed, never wanting to leave.

I stayed in that state of euphoria for about an hour. Then they yanked me from my warm cocoon and wheeled me to the surgery staging area. I found it very rude that they would share that delicious warmth with me only to replace it with harsh coldness. That staging area was frigid and there was no magical hose waiting there to warm me up.

While we waited in the surgical prep area, Mark and I were bombarded with questions and information from the surgical nurse who would be assisting in the surgery room. I was getting a bit restless and tried to be patient while she went over all the protocol items, but I really just wanted to get the show on the road.

Finally, things got rolling as the anesthesiologist came in to start my IV. He decided that the safest place for it would be in my foot. I could not have it anywhere on my right arm or hand because of the risk of lymphedema (due to the lymph node removal in my last surgery). My left arm was also out because of the work that they would be doing on that side of my body. So that left us with my foot, which was fine with me until he jabbed the needle into it. Yowza! I did not expect it to hurt fine with me until he jabbed the needle into it. Yowza! I did not expect it to hurt more than having it in my hand or arm, but it did.

After the anesthesiologist left, my surgeon, Dr. Leckman, stopped by to discuss his portion of the surgery. Then, my plastic surgeon, Dr. June Chen, came in to talk to us about her part in the surgery. She also used a Sharpie to draw all over my chest. That was a new experience for me, but it was necessary so that everything that needed to be removed would be, and everything that needed to stay would stay.

My surgery was going to be a skin-sparing bi-lateral mastectomy, performed by the very capable, Dr. Leckman. In this particular type of mastectomy, the surgeon can remove the breast tissue while keeping the breast skin and oftentimes, the nipples. Dr. Leckman was confident that this procedure would be the correct one for me and I felt good about it as well.

After Dr. Leckman had completed the mastectomy portion, it would be Dr. Chen's turn to begin the reconstruction process. That would involve inserting a tissue expander in each of my breasts. (Tissue expanders are evil, but more on that great adventure later.) When Dr. Chen completed her portion, it would be time for me to be wheeled to the recovery area.

I must pause for a moment and share with you the interesting experience that I had while writing this portion of my story. Up to this point, I had been good about writing details of everything that was happening to me, both in my journal and on my blog. But when I sat down to write about my mastectomy day, I realized that the details were not there.

I searched my chemo-clouded brain to come up with as many details as I could, but sadly, did not come up with many. Obviously, there was no way for me to know what went on while I was in surgery, and in the days that followed, I was on a lot of pain meds so that added to my cloudy brain.

That is when I turned to the Love of my Life, hoping that he could, once again, step in and save me. He could not remember specific details so he opened his journal to see if he had written anything there. What he found there amazed both of us. There, in his journal, was a detailed account of the entire surgery day.

He noted that it was strange to have that type of journal entry because normally, he did not write in his journal using such a specific timeline format. Was this a coincidence? I think not.

This experience was confirmation to me that this book needed to be written. There was no other explanation as to why Mark would suddenly choose to write such a detailed entry in his journal. Yes, this was most definitely not a coincidence.

The following is what he wrote:

"9:14 AM- I just got a call from the surgical nurse. Des is in surgery and things are progressing well. We got here at 6 AM. Des changed into her gown and was taken into the surgical prep area. Dr. Leckman came in and talked to us again about his part of the surgery. Finally, Dr. Chen came in and drew all over [Des'] chest to mark the areas she will work on. Then we had to separate.

It hadn't seemed real to me until we were sitting in the pre-op area. I haven't really been nervous or worried. However, sitting down there seeing her get prepped [for surgery], it hit me. I have almost lost her two times now. First, when [she was] pregnant with Josh and now with cancer. When I kissed her goodbye, my eyes welled up and [I continued to fight tears] as I walked down the hall to the waiting room. I know everything will be okay, but it is still hard to see someone you love have to face such a painful physical and emotional challenge. The surgery started at about 7:30 and should last for 4-5 hours.

10:10 AM- The nurse just called again. They have completed removing the left breast tissue and are beginning work on the right. Des is stable and doing well. It makes me sad to hear that the tissue is gone. It makes me sad for many reasons, but mostly because I know how this can affect Des' self-image.

She will have reconstruction, and she will look great, but it will be different. She has had so much sadness lately; I hate the fact that this will be a permanent reminder of this difficult year.

She told me the other day that several women in her support group had their husbands leave them after losing their hair or having a mastectomy. This has never crossed my mind. While I obviously enjoy the way her body looks, my love for her has absolutely no dependence on her appearance.

12:10 PM- Dr. Leckman just came out and told us (Des' mom has arrived to wait with me) that his part is done. He was very happy with how it went and felt like Des will be happy with the results. It was terrific news. I am relieved and very appreciative. He has been wonderful to us. He has never made us feel like he is rushed or needs to be someplace else. He has a very calm, reassuring manner and has always made us feel optimistic. What a wonderful blessing to have such a competent, caring man to help us through this scary situation.

Now [Des] is in Dr. Chen's hands. [Dr. Leckman mentioned that she is a perfectionist.] That means it will be a while still, but it will be done right. I have prayed many times, thanking my Heavenly Father, for blessing us to live in a time when we have the medical ability to cure this disease. Not many years ago it would have just been a matter of time until she became more and more ill as the cancer continued to spread until eventually killing her.

1:34 PM- I just received the latest update. They are closing up the incisions and Des is doing well. Dr. Chen should be out in 30-40 minutes to give me an update. Des' aunt Cheri is here now. She had her last chemo treatment just as Des was diagnosed. It has been good for Des to have her as a resource. She is a very loving person and has always made sure to give me a hug. She actually ran in the St. George marathon just a few months after completing her treatments. Des has to lie down after walking up the stairs. I don't know how anyone could run a marathon. What an amazing person.

10:00 PM- Des finally made it to her room around 4 PM. I could tell she was still very groggy from the anesthesia. Dr. Chen said everything looked really good. It took longer than planned because she participated in a study where they used contrast and a monitor to check blood flow. She was very nice and took the time to explain things to me. I tried to express to her how much I appreciated all her hard work to make sure the results were the best they could be.

I snuck out for a little while to get Des flowers and to grab a bite to eat. Val and Brian (co-workers) were nice enough to feed the kids by [taking them] five boxes of pizza! I couldn't believe how much there was, but Val wanted to make sure we had plenty of leftovers to eat. My co-workers have all been incredibly nice and supportive. I am blessed to have such a great job.

While I was out, a pretty big snowstorm started. Pauline (Des' mom) was going to bring the kids to visit, but both Des and I had separate, distinct impressions that she shouldn't come out in the weather. So we ended up Skyping with the kids instead.

I made it home about 8:30 PM... I am so happy the surgery went well. They were able to save Des' nipples, and both doctors seemed very happy with the results. I am very hopeful that my fears about her self-image will turn out to be unfounded. Either way, she is still here with me and we have the promise of a long, happy life together. I am so blessed."

Excuse me for a moment while I search for some tissues. I have an amazing husband. He is one of the many reasons that I fought so hard to live. We have a lot of living to do together and I am so grateful to have him by my side, now and throughout eternity. I could not have made it through this experience without him. Love you, honey. xoxo

~BRING IT ON~

Here I am on the day of my mastectomy, wearing the delicious gown
of magical warmth.
February 2012

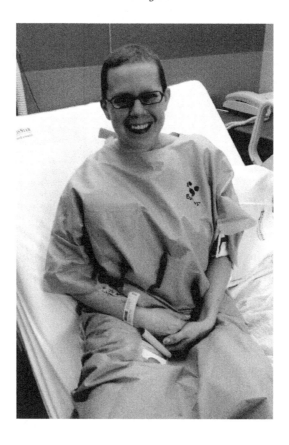

Twenty-Four: RECOVERY

My surgery required me to spend one night in the hospital. I was grateful that it was not more than that because that one night was extremely unpleasant. There was no sleep involved and my nurse was heavily overloaded with patients. Although she was trying her best to stay on top of things, my pain medication schedule took a back seat to her other responsibilities.

I have never been one who could block out pain. I took full advantage of the epidurals and other medications offered to me when I was delivering my children. When a headache starts creeping in, I immediately search for the Tylenol. I just don't have the mental prowess to allow myself to think of anything but the pain that my body is experiencing.

That night in the hospital was no exception. My body was hurting and I felt every uncomfortable sensation. It was a very long and frustrating night. I longed for the sun to peek its illustrious face in my window, ending my night-time of misery.

When the sun did arrive, I was so thankful. My nurse came by and apologized for her lack of attention to my needs. I expressed my forgiveness. After all, she was trying her best. She made sure that I had the appropriate medication and went to see what she could do about getting my check out process rolling.

I checked out of the hospital just after lunch and was so excited to be headed home. I have never been so happy to see my own bed. It had been calling me from miles away. As my head sank into my pillow, I sighed with contentment. It felt like heaven. I let the pain medication sleepiness take over, snuggled up with my own, familiar blanket, and slept for most of the afternoon.

Two days after my surgery, I turned 34 years old and received one of the best birthday presents ever. That present was a phone call from Dr. Leckman in which he told me that he had received the pathology reports back from the lab. Everything that had been sent in to be tested--my breast tissue samples and eight lymph nodes--came back with clear margins. In layman's terms, that meant no detectable traces of cancer. I cried for joy and Dr. Leckman said he was happy to be able to give me such a wonderful birthday present.

The rest of the day was spent partying, literally. We had Abbie's 8th birthday party scheduled for that afternoon. Who plans a big birthday party two days after major surgery? That would be me.

In our family, we only throw big birthday parties every four years. Since Abbie was turning 8, this was one of those party years. She had been looking forward to a party for a long time. I could not postpone or cancel it. She had already been through so much and had so many fun things canceled that I just could not add one more thing to that list. I enlisted the help of my mom, sister-in-law, niece, cousin, and friend and we put on the best Spa Day party any 8-year-old could ask for.

I looked and felt like I had been run over by a truck, multiple times, but I sat on the couch and soaked in the happy rays that were floating around in the party zone. I enjoyed every minute of the loudness, laughter, and chaos because I was still around to enjoy it.

Unfortunately, that euphoria did not last very long. Once I came down from the birthday party and pain medication cloud of happiness, the reality of my recovery process set in and I was utterly miserable.

I had expected to experience a lot of pain during recovery, and was correct in my assumption. As I fought to stay on top of the pain, I did have to remind myself that it could have been much worse. Because of the breast augmentation surgery that I had a few years earlier, my pectoral muscles were already stretched out. That proved to be helpful in two ways:

For one thing, it allowed Dr. Chen to be able to fill the tissue expanders with a small amount of saline solution during my surgery. That was not a normal procedure to have happen during that initial reconstruction surgery. It would have been too much for those muscles to handle. However, because my muscles were relaxed enough, I was able to have some saline injected, which meant that I did not wake up to a concave chest after my surgery. Instead, I woke up being just a few sizes smaller than I originally had been. It was a blessing to not have to go through the shock of looking down to see a caved-in chest.

Secondly, my muscles were not as sore as they could have been. Although there was a lot of pain going on, it was not as much as it should have been. I had already experienced that excruciating pain when I went through the breast augmentation recovery in 2009. It had been a nightmare to go through that pain then, but I was so grateful that I didn't have to go through it again, considering the weakened state that my chemo-riddled body was in.

Aside from the pain I was experiencing, I had other factors that were causing a huge amount of discomfort and overall annoyance. There were three factors to be exact--my surgical drains. Beautifully disgusting surgical drains.

When you have a mastectomy, the doctor usually places surgical drains in your chest to assist with the healing process. They are designed to relieve pressure by draining excess fluid.

As I mentioned before, I had to have three drains--two in the right side of my chest and one on the left. Each drain consisted of a long piece of tubing that protruded out of my rib cage area. The tubing was held in place with a few stitches, which were horribly itchy. At the end of the tubing, there was a bulb syringe with a little cap on top of it. The syringe needed to be kept flat, with no air in it, so that it could act as a vacuum and pull out all the excess fluid from the surgical sites.

I had one job with the drains and that was to keep track of how much fluid was draining out each day. So twice a day, I would uncap the syringes and carefully pour the liquid into a measuring cup. The liquid started out a little on the bloody side and eventually turned a sickish yellow color. Can you say, "Disgusting?" It was one of the most unpleasant things I have ever had to do and I have had to face a lot of disgusting situations as the mother of four children.

I wish I could say that the annoyance of the drains was the only hiccup from my mastectomy. Au contraire. Only two days after my surgery, I noticed that my right arm looked and felt a little swollen. I had a post-op appointment with Dr. Chen that day so she checked it out.

She determined that the swelling could be from several issues, such as lymphedema setting in, a blood clot, or just some random swelling from the trauma of surgery. She told me to watch it closely over the weekend and to call Dr. Leckman if the swelling had not gone down by Monday.

Not only did my upper arm stay swollen all weekend, but the swelling continued to travel down my arm. By Monday, my whole arm was swollen. Mark insisted on calling me "Popeye." I was not amused.

I called Dr. Leckman and he scheduled me for an ultrasound to see if there was a blood clot prowling around in there. As I was lying on the cold, hard table in the ultrasound room, with my right arm dangling crazily at an uncomfortable angle, I did some more pleading with God.

"Please don't let there be any blood clots. I don't think I can handle any complications right now."

My prayer was answered in one way because the ultrasound tech did not see any blood clots. Whew! I definitely dodged a bullet there. Unfortunately, the ultrasound did not give us any clues as to why my arm was swelling up like a balloon, so the complication potential climbed a few notches.

The following day I went in to see Dr. Leckman for my post-op appointment. I was hoping to be able to have my drains removed while I was there.

I had been diligent in keeping an accurate drainage record and knew that two of the drains had reached the drainage goal of 20 cc's or less.

He did remove those two well-behaved drains, which was a huge relief and one of the strangest sensations I have ever experienced. First, he cut the stitches around the tubing (ouch). Then he gently pulled on the tube. I was amazed at how much of that tubing was inside my body! I felt like I was a magician's assistant and Dr. Leckman was performing the never-ending handkerchief routine. Finally, the end of the tubing came and I was free, from two of the drains at least.

Once he had placed bandages over the holes so they could heal properly, he sat down to discuss the other issue that I had...meaning, my "Popeye" arm. After examining it and reading through the ultrasound report, he determined that Lymphedema had set in. Great. That was not something that was a part of my "road to recovery" plan.

Lymphedema can happen any time you have lymph nodes removed. I had a total of ten lymph nodes removed between my lumpectomy and mastectomy. This had created a disturbance in my lymphatic system. (The lymphatic system is a network of vessels and nodes that help keep bodily fluid levels in balance and it also helps your body wage war against infection.) With ten of my nodes suddenly MIA (Missing in Action), my body did not know what to do with the fluid in my arm and the result was my condition of "Popeye arm."

Now, the lymphatic system is pretty smart in the fact that it can reroute and find another way to process things. Sometimes, it just needs a little help in doing that. That is where a Lymphedema specialist comes in. For those of you who are keeping track, my doctor count now consisted of a Gynecologist, a Surgeon, a Plastic Surgeon, an Oncologist, a Radiation Oncologist (whom I haven't mentioned yet), and a Lymphedema specialist.

My Lymphedema expert was the lovely Barbara. She was a patient of Dr. Leckman's and a breast cancer survivor as well, so we had some things in common. I met with her on the day after my appointment with Dr. Leckman.

She began by taking measurements of the circumference of my arm, from wrist to shoulder. Those measurements would help us keep track of the progress we hoped to make as my arm swelling decreased. Then, she gave me the "Welcome to Life with Lymphedema" speech. Again, I was not amused.

Living with Lymphedema had the potential to be a very unpleasant experience. For example:

*Initially I would need to meet with Barbara twice a week for three months. Now, don't get me wrong, I liked talking with Barbara and she was a very nice person, but the thought of adding that many appointments to a lengthy list of appointments that I already had, was very overwhelming. Barbara did say that if everything went well, we might be about to shave the time down to two months. I immediately started praying that my arm would respond well so we could lose that extra month of appointments.

*I would now need to start wearing a compression sleeve all the time. I could take it off to shower or go swimming, but at least for now, it would become a permanent addition to my wardrobe.

*She suggested limiting my salt intake. Too much salt equals too much fluid in your body.

*I would need to be careful not to get too many cuts, scratches, or bug bites on my right arm. They could possibly open the door to infections. Hmm. I had the thought, "*How do I tell a bug not to bite my right arm? Do you think bugs can read medical alert bracelets?*"

*I would need to be careful about carrying too many heavy things with my right arm. Great, now my left arm would start to look like Popeye's arm because it would be doing all the work from now on.

*As I mentioned earlier in the book, I would not be able to have shots, IV's, or blood pressure cuffs on my right arm. All those things could cause the lymphedema to flare up.

After the speech, Barbara set to work performing a lymphatic massage to my arm to help reroute the lymph system. I stared up at the ceiling trying to process all the information she had just jammed down my throat.

I didn't want to have to worry about Lymphedema for the rest of my life! My thoughts turned to summertime and how it would be to have to wear a restricting compression sleeve in the blistering heat. Couldn't I just return to my life before cancer? The life where I didn't have to worry about things like chemo side effects, surgery recovery, drains not cooperating, and "Popeye arms?"

––

"Day 207: Today was another uncomfortable, semi-hard day. My hair is coming in nicely and I have not been wearing many scarves or hats.

Of course, I have mostly been at home, but I have ventured out to a few stores [without covering] my little round head. It has been

okay. I feel like people are staring, [although] I know that I am being hypersensitive about it and that not everybody is staring at me. It was almost easier to have the crutch of wearing the scarf, once I got used to it. When I went out, people could look at me and see that I have cancer or some other medical issue. Now I just [look like] I have a weird haircut.

I don't really feel like wearing the scarves, or even hats anymore. I think there are two reasons for that.

1. I am sick of them. I have no desire to [wear them] anymore.

2. As I was sitting in Relief Society today, pondering about this new step in the journey, a thought came to me. I think on some subconscious level, I associate the scarves and hats with cancer. I wore those when I had cancer. I don't have cancer anymore. It's gone--outta here--see ya--ba bye. So now that I don't have cancer, I am not interested in wearing the scarves, not on my head anyway...

I am starting to feel a bit better every day. My left nipple is having some issues. It's very raw. Not sure if it is from wearing the [surgical recovery] bra all the time or something else. I have to keep it bandaged or it just bleeds everywhere.

I also think that I might have a little infection or something where one of my drains was. I am keeping that bandaged up as well. My one remaining drain is slowing down, but still has [too much] fluid draining. I hope it slows down more so [Dr. Chen] can take it out at my appointment on Tuesday...

Celebrating my 34th birthday and the good news that I was officially cancer free. March 2012

Twenty-Five:

MY NEW ENEMY

As if dealing with an ornery drain was not enough of a challenge, I was also fighting with another new nemesis in my life: the evil tissue expanders. A tissue expander is a type of breast implant that is used to create space in your breast while you undergo radiation treatment. From what I understand, it is not wise to go through radiation with regular saline or silicone-filled implants. One of the possible side effects from radiation is a change in your skin's elasticity, which greatly affects how an implant would look and feel under your skin. For this reason, my doctor recommended the tissue expanders.

In my limited medical knowledge, I am aware of two differences between the tissue expanders and a regular breast implant. One of those differences is that on the top of the expander, there is a tiny valve mechanism. That is used when it is time to go through the "expansion process" in which the expander is slowly filled with saline. The saline causes the expander to enlarge, which results in your skin and muscle stretching to create and hold a space large enough for your desired size of implants. The other difference is that the expanders are as hard as a rock.

~MY NEW ENEMY~

From my own experience with tissue expanders, I have come up with another use for them: torture devices. If you ever want to get information from someone, just sign them up for a couple of tissue expanders and start filling those babies up with saline. That person will give you any information you want, guaranteed.

Before my mastectomy, I talked with other breast cancer survivors about what to expect from the surgery and expanders. I quickly came to this conclusion: tissue expanders are terrible, awful, painful, and by far, the worst part of the reconstruction process. My tissue expander enemies lived up to every expectation I had for them, and then some.

After recovering from my mastectomy for about two weeks, I went to Dr. Chen's office to have my second saline expansion. Since the first expansion was completed during my surgery, I did not know what was involved or how it would feel.

As I waited for Dr. Chen with one octopus-like drain still clinging to my right side, I felt my anxiety level rising. My senses were suddenly acutely aware of the frigid air in the room, the rigidity of the procedure chair I was sitting on, and the paper-thin nature of the rose-colored gown I was wearing.

"Oh, I hope this is going to be a relatively painless process!" I silently pleaded. After the ups and downs of the diagnosis, chemotherapy, surgery, and recovery, I didn't know how much more my mind and body could take.

Dr. Chen came in, we exchanged pleasantries and then she got down to business. Even though I was extremely nervous, I found the procedure fascinating. First, she cleaned my chest, making it as sterile as possible. Then she pulled out a teardrop-shaped device with a round opening in the center. In this opening, there was a magnet. Dr. Chen explained that the magnet would tell her where the metal valve on the tissue expander was located so that she would know where to insert the needle to inject the saline.

She swiped the device over the top of my breasts in a circular motion. When the magnet stopped moving, she knew she had found the valve. A marker was used to mark the correct spot and then she turned to her little metal tray of

123

supplies. When she turned back around, she was clasping a syringe in her hands. It was then that I started to feel sick.

The syringe was not the problem. The problem was the gigantic needle that was protruding from the top of that syringe. Umm...surely you are not planning on sticking that into my boobs? It's a good thing the mastectomy made me completely numb in that region of my body. I was positive that if I had feeling there, I would not like what was about to happen. Dr. Chen continued her explanation of what was going to happen next.

"Typically, I like to do at least 60 cc's of saline during each expansion appointment. However, if you feel all right after the 60 cc's, we could always do more."

Sixty cc's doesn't sound like much, right? It also did not look like much as she carefully filled the syringe with saline. When the syringe was ready to go, I quickly turned my head so I wouldn't have to see her plunge the needle into the top of my right breast.

I felt like a cartoon character as the saline flowed into my expander and my breast started to slowly expand. It was kind of a cool, yet extremely weird feeling. Once the right breast was filled with 60 cc's, it was time for the left breast.

"How are you feeling?" Dr. Chen asked once the left breast fill was completed.

"Well, considering that I just had a giant needle stuck in me and watched my breasts fill up like a water balloon, I think I feel okay," I was thinking.

"I feel fine," is what I replied.

"Would you like to go for another 60 cc's? That might be all we need to do and then you wouldn't need to come back for another expansion," she said.

I pondered the decision for a few moments. Every other survivor I had talked to told me to go slowly with the expansion process. "Take your time and you won't regret it," they said. Now, here I was, all prepped and ready. The thought of having one less doctor's appointment must have clouded my judgment and all the sound advice I had received flew right out the window.

Since I wasn't experiencing any pain from the first 60 cc's and the process wasn't nearly as bad as I thought it would be, why not go for the extra sixty? I convinced myself that it would be a great thing to do and told Dr. Chen to go for it.

I regretted my decision midway through the second fill. That's when the pain started. I also started experiencing a strange sensation like I was being pushed to the ground and held there by an elephant. I couldn't catch my breath. As the room started to spin, I quickly closed my eyes.

"How are you doing?" Dr. Chen asked.

"Fine," I squeaked. (If you consider *fine* as being suffocated by an elephant.) I guess I thought I was being heroic. What was my problem? Why would I not tell Dr. Chen how I was really feeling?

I knew that we couldn't turn back now. Not with one side of me 60 cc's bigger than the other side. I was already mostly bald, eyebrow-less, and looked like I had been run over by a truck. I did not need to add being lopsided to that list of stunning features. In went 60 more cc's to the left breast. Same story, different breast. Suffocation by an elephant in full force.

"Okay. That about does it," Dr. Chen said. "Do you need any more pain meds? You will be a little sore for a few days."

"Huh? What? Are you talking to me? Because I can't hear you. I am focusing on breathing in and out right now."

"Nope," I replied. "I am good. I still have meds at home."

I just wanted to get out of there as fast as my legs would take me. It was possibly one of the dumbest mistakes I had made on my journey. Had I only expressed to Dr. Chen how I was feeling at that moment, she would have been able to remove the extra saline and everything would have been fine. But my desire to feel in control and move the process along won, no matter how dumb it was. I was really wishing that I had taken my mother-in-law's offer for her to drive me to the appointment.

She knew how I would be feeling because she had been there, done that. But, I had to be the hero; the one who could do it by herself. Had I learned nothing about the value of accepting help when it was offered? Apparently, yes, I had not.

Dr. Chen left the room so I could get dressed. Once the door closed I thought, "*How in the world am I going to get my shirt on?*" I could barely move without searing pain shooting through my numb chest. You know that you are in a bad situation when most of the nerve endings have been severed, but you *still* feel pain.

Somehow, I managed to get out of the pink gown and into my shirt. Tears started to form as I tried to gather up my belongings. I felt paralyzed, unable to make any quick movements or slow movements for that matter. Everything that I did produced pain, even blinking back my tears.

I slowly made my way out of the room and said goodbye to the people at the front desk, hoping they would not notice my distress. I did not want any attention drawn to me because I did not want to stay in that office one minute longer. I just wanted to go home, find my pain meds, and not move for three days.

I finally made it to my van, still angry with myself for not allowing my mother-in-law to drive me. At that point, I could not see how I was going to drive myself home in the condition I was in. It hurt to breathe. It hurt to move and I could not move my arms very well.

I sat in the driver's seat and cried. What have I done? *"Get back into Dr. Chen's office and tell her what is going on!"* I screamed to myself. Nope. Still have the martyr complex going on. How about I call my husband instead?

When Mark answered his phone, I unloaded on him.

"I feel like I have two enormous watermelons strapped to my chest! I can't breathe! I can't move! I don't know how I am going to drive home!"

"What can I do?" he asks. "Do you need me to come get you and we can pick up the van later?"

"No. I will be fine," I replied. Again, with the martyr stuff! What was my problem? "I will call you when I get home."

I prayed the entire drive home and my prayer was answered because somehow, I made it home without injuring myself or others. Once I made it into the house, I planted myself on the couch and did not move for the rest of the afternoon.

~MY NEW ENEMY~

"WOW!! I thought that surgery was going to be the most painful part of this whole process. Nope. I was wrong. Getting more saline put into my tissue expander was the most painful...The pain that I have experienced this afternoon is the same pain that I went through three years ago when I had the implants, [only worse.]

It hurts to move, breathe, laugh, [and] sneeze...I am so thankful that I had the implants though. That is going to make it so that this may be my only expansion...We will see what they look like next week. So, it's back to the strong pain meds. I don't know how I am going to sleep tonight. I can tell you right now that there is no way I will be able to find a comfortable position. Have I mentioned that cancer sucks?"

That night is on my list of "The Longest Nights of my Life." There was no comfortable position to be found. Somewhere in the middle of the night the tight, heavy, "being suffocated by an elephant" feeling left, but it was replaced with pain; searing, intense, insane pain. It was like nothing that I have ever felt before.

I spent the next day mostly on the couch, with as little food and potty breaks as I could get away with. About three days after my expansion, I felt like I could rejoin the land of the living. The pain had subsided a bit and I was able to move around a little easier.

I went to a follow-up appointment with Dr. Chen so we could address the issue of my "third arm"--my last remaining surgical drain. It was supposed to have been removed weeks earlier with the other drains, but instead, it was following me around like Mary's obnoxious little lamb.

Unfortunately, my right breast was still draining too much fluid and was covered in a big, nasty bruise. It had now been just over two weeks since my surgery. I had passed the point where most women are able to be free from their drains but I had no prospect of losing this one any time soon. Drat. Now I have to take the stupid thing with me on my upcoming trip.

As part of my birthday present, I had plans to head to Phoenix with Mark. His work was having a retreat/business conference there and I was lucky enough

127

to be able to join him. I thought it would be the perfect opportunity for me to bask in the sun and take a break from the past few months of insanity.

I really, REALLY did not want to have my "third arm" tag along. Trust me. No one would want me hanging out by him or her at the pool. I would be the crazy bald lady with a bulb full of gross fluid dangling from her body. Not a pretty picture.

Although I was extremely disappointed that the drain could not come out, I decided that I needed to start counting my blessings. I was still experiencing a small amount of pain, but at least it wasn't going to prevent me from going on the trip. Everything was looking up for the moment.

That's when my bad luck fairy swooped in and I was reminded that I was not in charge.

Twenty-Six:

THE PHOENIX MIRACLE

It was a Friday night. Day 212. The night before we were to leave for our Phoenix trip. I felt a little feverish and my legs started aching right before bedtime. A million possibilities ran through my head, but I chalked them up to the chemo still trying to work its way out of my body so I just put myself to bed a little early. I wanted to be as rested as possible for our big travel day.

Around midnight I woke up in complete agony. I still felt hot, but cold at the same time. The pain that I had been experiencing since my expansion had not only returned, but had increased in magnitude. My whole upper body was wracked with pain. Once again, it hurt to breathe, move, or even stay still. My pain medication was not even touching it. The only thing that the meds accomplished was that they made me sleepier. That added to my frustration because I was in so much pain that I couldn't find a comfortable position in which to fall asleep.

I toughed it out until 7 A.M. and then decided that I should ask for help because I couldn't stand the pain any longer. I crawled from the living room to my bedroom and clung to Mark's side of our bed. I woke him up and begged him to call his dad to see if he would be willing to come over to assist Mark in giving me a priesthood blessing. I had been praying all night long and now I felt like I needed a little extra help. I had done all that I could do and I was completely exhausted.

All the fatigue, frustration, and pain collided and I burst into sobs. The muscles in my chest felt like someone was twisting them, wringing them out like a sponge. On top of that, a new pain in the upper right side of my back had surfaced somewhere in the middle of the night, taking my malaise to a new level.

Mark quickly got out of bed and called his parents. They rushed right over so that I could receive a blessing. A priesthood blessing of healing consists of two parts--one to anoint the person's head with consecrated oil and another to seal the anointing and offer words of comfort. Typically, Mark would always seal the anointing, but this time he asked his dad if he would perform the sealing. Later, when I asked him why he thought to have his dad perform the sealing, he said that he just felt like his dad should be the one to do it.

My wonderful father-in-law gave me a beautiful blessing of healing, peace, and comfort. He told me to seek for help from the medical professionals that I trusted and that they would know what to do to help me. He also said that my pain would be managed and that I would still be able to go on my trip as planned and have a relaxing time.

To those of you outside of my religion, the concept of a priesthood blessing might sound a bit confusing or, to choose another word, weird. I get it. I wish that I could explain it better. All I can tell you is this: I believe that the same priesthood that Christ held when He was living on the Earth has been restored, and we are able to access that priesthood today. As Elders in our church, my husband and father-in-law hold this priesthood that allows them the opportunity to give blessings. Although it was my father-in-law who was speaking during my blessing, I know that the words were from God. I also felt that God had cried with me on many occasions, that He was fully aware of the pain that I had been experiencing, and He was concerned for my well being.

After the blessing, I called Dr. Chen. It was so good to hear her voice. She gently scolded me by telling me that I should have called her sooner. She felt badly that I had suffered through the night. I knew that she was right. However, during the night, I kept thinking that I would be turning a corner at any moment and that the pain would miraculously just go away on its own. I also had not wanted to bother her so late at night.

Dr. Chen instructed me to go to the ER so that they could check me for blood clots or a kidney infection. Those were not possibilities that I wanted to hear. It was now 7:30 A.M. and Mark and I were supposed to be to the airport by noon. But, as much as I hated to admit it, I knew that we had to go to the ER. I could hardly stand up straight. There was no way that I would be able to tolerate a flight in my condition. Plus, the possibility of a blood clot in my lungs or an infection in my kidneys was freaking me out. Reluctantly, we gathered up a few items and drove to the hospital.

Fortunately, it was a slow morning at the ER and we were taken right back to a room. The doctor came in to assess me and she ordered some blood work, a chest x-ray, and a chest CT. She also ordered one more thing...Mr. Morphine. Yes, please, and thank you.

As the medication flowed into my veins I had a realization of how someone could become addicted to morphine. Where my body had been consumed with horrendous pain, suddenly it was absorbed with mind-numbing relief and it felt wonderful. After five days of near constant pain, I was finally able to relax. I still couldn't make any quick movements because I would get a stab of pain, but it was nothing compared to what I had been experiencing just a few hours earlier.

Mark and I began to think that maybe we would be able to catch our flight after all. So far everything had been moving so quickly. Maybe luck would be on our side that day.

We shouldn't have let ourselves get hopeful. After the morphine was administered, we waited and waited for them to come and take me for the x-ray and chest CT. All the while, watching the clock move closer and closer to the time when we were supposed to check in at the airport.

Finally, an orderly came and took me for a chest x-ray and CT scan. I remember nothing from either of those because of my altered morphine state of mind. However, I do remember the doctor coming in a little while later with the good news.

"Guess what? You are fine! We didn't find anything out of the ordinary on the x-ray or the CT. No blood clot or kidney infection. Everything looks great. You must just be experiencing some residual pain from your surgery and expansion. Here are some more pain meds. Have fun on your trip!"

And just as quickly as she had appeared, she bustled off again, on to the next waiting patient. Mark and I were obviously relieved with the good news, but also a little confused as to why I had been experiencing such intense pain. Still, we trusted that the doctor and radiologist knew what they were talking about so we gathered up our things and headed to the car.

We drove out of the hospital parking lot just in time to miss our flight to Arizona. To add insult to injury, the morphine was wearing off and my irritable friend, Ms. Pain, was trying to weasel her way back in.

As we headed to the pharmacy to pick up my prescription, Mark tried to call the airline to see what our options were since we had missed our flight. They told him that there was a later flight that we might be able to get on, but he would need to call back at 5 P.M. to see if there was any space available.

By the time we arrived home, my mom was there. She had come to stay with our kids while we were out of town. Everything seemed to be falling back into place. We had my pain sort of figured out, our bags were almost packed, and our kids were taken care of. All we had to do was wait until five o'clock to call the airline and get on the later flight.

At 5 P.M. on the dot, Mark called the airline. That was when the world came crashing down once again.

"Oh, I'm sorry," the customer service agent said, "There are no seats available on that flight."

You have got to be kidding me. I waited for Mark to tell me that he was joking, but the confession never came. He was put on hold while the agent checked out some other options. A few minutes later, she came back on the line with some great news.

"Good news!" she said. "It looks like one seat has opened up!"

One seat. Wow, that was...not good news. Saying that I was devastated would be a large understatement. I knew what *my* option was at this point. Staying home. Mark was the one who needed to be in Arizona, not me.

With every ounce of courage I could muster, I told him to just take the one available seat and cancel my ticket. At least, I tried to say that. I was mid-sentence when the waterworks started and I had to excuse myself. I went into our closet, shut the door, and burst into tears.

I tried not to cry too loudly because Mark was still on the phone with the airline. I was crying quietly enough to hear him say that he would take the ticket and just cancel mine. That's when I really lost it. I am talking heaving, "my world has just ended" sobs.

Never mind the fact that with each gulp of breath I received a shooting pain in my chest. At that point, I didn't care. I was angry, sad, and frustrated. I felt very childlike and silly for the behavior that I was exhibiting, but I couldn't help myself. The disappointment was heart wrenching.

Then my sweetheart of a husband did something that should be recorded in the annals of all things chivalrous. He heard the great commotion that was happening in the closet (to be honest, the neighbors had probably heard me sobbing), and said these words to the lady on the phone.

"I can't take that ticket. I can't leave my wife behind. I will have to figure something else out. Thank you, anyway."

Well, if I wasn't crying hard enough before, hearing those words sent me right over the edge.

I hugged him as tightly as my pain-riddled chest would allow. The good news was, I had an awesome husband who would not leave his bald, sobbing, "still has a gross drain hanging out of her side" wife behind. What a saint! I am sure that there are plenty of men who would have looked for any excuse to get away from the hideousness of that reality.

The bad news was that he needed to be in Arizona and at the current moment, we had no good way to get him there. We did have the option to drive, but that would mean canceling both tickets and paying a hefty fine. There was also news of a winter storm brewing in the very direction that we would need to be driving. That option was not fun or safe.

We debated about what to do and then I finally just told him that he needed to call the airline back to see if that one ticket was still available. I would just have to put on my big girl pants and deal with it.

I know that Mark felt torn. He didn't want to leave me when he knew that I was so sad and in a lot of physical pain, but he had an obligation that needed to be fulfilled. It was at this point in time that I felt a sudden surge of hatred for the ugly cancer monster. Hadn't we been through enough over the past seven months? Didn't we deserve a small break from the chaos?

For the first time, I was truly furious with cancer and I let that anger take me down a road I had not wanted to travel. I had never uttered the words "it's not fair" regarding my journey. I had learned so much and experienced so many tender mercies. But the physical pain, sheer exhaustion, and the fading prospect of a weekend away from it all became too much to bear. I found myself screaming, *"IT'S JUST NOT FAIR!"* in my mind.

I stayed in the closet, wallowing in a well-deserved moment of self-pity while Mark got back on the phone with the airline. It was then that we were blessed with a miracle. As Mark was explaining the situation again, he learned that while we were discussing things, and while I was having my major meltdown, another seat had opened up. There were now two available seats on that flight.

I was instantly humbled and brought to tears (again), but those tears were ones of joy. I knew that I had just witnessed another miracle. As silly as it seemed and as childish as I felt, my Heavenly Father understood those feelings. He knew that I just needed to get away for a few days. It was important to me, so that made it important to Him and our prayer was answered.

We touched down in Arizona a few hours later and I shuffled off the plane as fast as my tired legs could carry me. My pain medication was wearing off and I just wanted to get to the resort, get in my pajamas, and go to bed.

After an uncomfortable ride in our rental car, we pulled up to the resort and, you guessed it, the tears started again. It was so peaceful and beautiful!

From the fountains flowing with water that sparkled in the setting sun, to the tropical foliage that enveloped us like a warm blanket, I fell completely in love with the place. It would be the perfect place for me to refuel, relax, and to gear up for the next stage of my battle.

Twenty-Seven: THE DRAIN THAT WOULD NOT QUIT

Our time in Arizona would have been perfect except for two things. First, I was still in a huge amount of pain. It hurt to move. It hurt to sit still. It hurt to lie down. The only way I could achieve comfort at night was to sit fully upright in a chair. I fashioned a little fort of pillows around me to support my head and neck. By doing this I managed to catch a few hours of sleep (or something that resembled sleep.)

The second thing that hindered my ability to fully relax was the discomfort from my remaining surgical drain. Blast that drain! It was a huge pain in my side--literally. Being that it was way past the obnoxious point, I was ready to yank it out myself. Unfortunately, it was still draining more than 40 cc's of fluid every day. Although the fluid had changed from being tinged with blood to a sickly yellow color, there was still too much of it to meet the requirement for removal.

Once we arrived home, I felt the rage and regret move in. Maybe this whole reconstruction jazz was a mistake. I mean, who needs boobs anyway? They just get in the way, and sometimes, they try to kill you. Why was I putting myself through such misery?

I had reached the end of my patience rope and I went to my next appointment with Dr. Chen ready to do <u>anything</u> if she would just remove the drain or maybe get rid of my entire right breast altogether. I could not stand the pain and discomfort one second longer. It was excruciating nearly every minute, day and night.

"Dr. Chen was concerned that I was still in so much pain. [She was also worried because] the stuff coming out of my drain looks infected. But I haven't had a fever and my breast does not have [classic] infection symptoms. She took 40 cc's of saline out, [hoping that it would relieve some pressure and pain.] Then she pushed and poked, trying to direct some of the fluid to the drain. All the while I am moaning and flinching. She put me on some antibiotics and I have to go back in on Tuesday."

Something else that Dr. Chen mentioned at that appointment was that if the drain did not start slowing down soon, or there were any changes to the look of my breast, she would have to remove the tissue expander and start the process over again. She suggested that I take it easy for a few days to see if I could get the fluid to slow down.

I decided that it was time to declare war on my new enemy (AKA the tissue expander from the underworld.) If it meant that I had to sit on my couch and do nothing for a week straight, I would do it. I was desperate and so exhausted. Although I could sneak in little catnaps here and there, I had not had a full night's sleep since before my surgery. The lack of sleep added to my lack of patience causing me to be a tad unpleasant to be around.

Day 230: "I still have this very annoying drain...It is very old. It's a nuisance. It itches, and hurts when I bump it. It is starting to leak [around the tubing that is protruding from my rib cage.] I am really trying to be patient, but it is hard.

At this point in the journey, I feel kind of numb. I feel like I am just going through the motions [again.] I have some sort of doctor's appointment at least two times a week. I think if you added up how much time I have spent in doctor's offices over the past 230 days, it would easily equal about one full month (or more) of my life. I can't start radiation until my drain is out, so once again, I am playing the waiting game. Stuck in limbo."

Day 235: "Still in limbo. Still mostly uncomfortable, especially at night. I feel like this drain is never going to go away. It has slowed down a tiny bit today, but not enough to get it out. I should get a prize or something for being the one with the drain in the longest.

It has now been 40 days since my surgery. Usually drains are in for 14-21 days. I just want to move on! But...things happen for a reason. Maybe my body just needs some extra time to heal before it takes another beating [with radiation] ...

Today was Easter and it was another gorgeous day outside. I love the springtime. The trees all look amazing and there is such a wonderful crisp, new smell in the air. Perfect for my fresh start on life. Gone is the dreary winter with its sickness and yuckiness. It is replaced with the wonderful hope of a bright future as I move forward and try to live my life better."

Day 241: "...I have still spent the week with this obnoxious drain. [Making it 46 days since surgery.] I have decided that it is coming out on Tuesday even if I have to [alter] the numbers a bit. [The drainage] has stayed between 30-40 cc's for almost a month now. It's not going any lower. I have pretty much been in bed all weekend, and it hasn't slowed down any. So I will be telling Dr. Chen that it has stayed below 30 for a few days. I can't bear it anymore and I want to get started with radiation...

It's hard to believe that this whole journey is nearing an end. It feels like yesterday that I was holding my phone to my ear, listening to someone tell me that I have cancer. I will never forget that moment. The initial shock and disbelief. Trying to hold back my tears and be brave for my girls. I have learned so much about myself, and [just] life in general. I wouldn't trade the things that I have learned, but I hope to never have to experience this again in my lifetime."

Twenty-Eight:
THE NEVER-ENDING STORY

By this time, I felt like a hamster on a wheel. I just kept running and running but I was getting absolutely nowhere. I could see the final destination in front of me, but I just could not get there.

Finally, on Day 245, I was able to escape the wheel. After seven very long weeks, my drain was removed. I had truly learned the meaning of the word "loath." I loathed that drain and I was beyond ready to move on to the next step in kicking cancer out of my life. Getting rid of that appendage created a huge amount of excitement and relief.

Unfortunately for me, my body still had some surprises in store. Don't get me wrong. I like surprises when they come in the form of a party or something fun like that. However, I <u>do not</u> like surprises when they come in the form of a massive infection in my breast.

My drain was removed on a Tuesday afternoon. By Wednesday my right breast was swollen and a little tender. I had an appointment scheduled for Thursday morning with my Radiation Oncologist. I decided that I would just let her take a look at it and then go from there.

I prayed non-stop from Wednesday evening to Thursday morning. *"Please! Please let this be nothing. Please let the swelling go down. Please let her say that it's still okay to start radiation."*

I didn't feel like I could face another setback. I just had to get going with radiation because I absolutely needed to be free from the chain of cancer. It was a chain that I felt was being lengthened instead of shortened--chink by agonizing chink.

Unfortunately, this was going to be one of those times where my will was obviously not God's will, which happens more often than not, actually. You would think that I would have learned that lesson by now.

My radiation doctor (Dr. Avizonis) took one look at my swollen breast, which by now was twice the size of my left one, and said, "I'm sorry. It's a no go. We need to figure out why that breast is so swollen."

I was crushed. I had already given up eight months of my life to cancer. I was now seven weeks beyond what I had planned in my own "kicking cancer to the curb" timeline. I couldn't bear the thought of adding more time.

After shedding more than a few tears in the car, I regained my composure and called Dr. Chen to see what she wanted me to do. It just so happened to be a surgery day for her, so she was not in the office. I told the nurse what was happening and she said she would try to contact Dr. Chen and get back to me. When she did call me back, I was surprised at what Dr. Chen needed me to do.

"Since Dr. Chen is in surgery," the nurse explained, "she was wondering if you could take a picture of your breast and email it to the office. I will then forward it to her and she can take a look and let us know what she wants you to do."

"Umm, excuse me? You want me to take a picture of my breast and then email it to you? Have it out there in cyberspace?"

Well, I guess I can add that to the list of firsts that cancer has brought into my life; emailing someone a picture of my breast. For a very conservative gal like me, it was a highly uncomfortable situation. What other choice did I have though? My breast seemed to be expanding by the minute and my skin felt like it was at its breaking point.

After weighing the options in my mind, I decided that if taking a picture of my breast was what I needed to do to make things happen, then that is what I would do.

I rushed home as fast as I could and barricaded myself in my bathroom. I grabbed my phone and took my boob's first, and last, selfie. I hit the send button and waited for Dr. Chen's assistant to get back to me. In the meantime, I erased the picture from my phone. I was mortified to think that someone (like one of my kiddos) would ever take my phone, start flipping through my pictures, and stumble across that beauty. That had awkward written all over it.

I received a call back a few hours later. Dr. Chen was on her way back to her office and wanted to see me right away. It was about 5 P.M. I felt badly that she had been in surgery all day and was now making a special trip back to the office to see me and my troublemaker boob, but I had to know what the next step would be.

Surprisingly I was pretty calm when I walked into her office. It was another one of those times where I know that I was being carried by unseen hands. It was the only way to explain the lack of a major meltdown.

Once again, I found myself sitting in a rose-colored gown, waiting to be seen by Dr. Chen. When she came into the room, she sat down across from me and opened the front of my gown. Before she had even opened it all the way she said, "You need surgery and you need it tonight. We have to get that expander out of there. There is definitely an infection going on."

Wait a second here. Surgery? Right now? That was not on my list of things to do! I haven't prepared for that! I was supposed to be starting radiation, not throwing in an unplanned surgery. Yet again, I was given a not-so-subtle reminder that I was not the one in charge.

Mark and I left her office and scrambled to do what was needed to make sure that we had everything we would need for a night in the hospital. We also had to find someone to take care of our kids. Fortunately, both of those tasks were completed quickly and we were off to the hospital within an hour.

I still felt calm, but I think some of that calm feeling was because I was in shock. All my movements felt sluggish, like I was moving in a dream. I couldn't remember anything, including important details like what or when I had eaten last. Did I have a salad for lunch? Yes, that sounds right. Did I eat anything after that? I couldn't remember.

It was as though the last few hours of my life had not happened and I could not make my brain remember anything beyond the words, "You need surgery."

After checking in at the hospital, I was taken to the frigid surgery area. My IV was in position and I was about five minutes away from surgery when the anesthesiologist asked me the dreaded question.

"When did you eat last?"

At Dr. Chen's office, I was confident that the last thing I had eaten was my salad for lunch. Unfortunately, somewhere in between the check in process and the IV placement, I realized that I had eaten a handful of pretzels on my way out the door when I left to pick up the kids from school.

Everything came to a screeching halt. In order to have surgery, you need to wait at least six hours after you have eaten anything--unless it's an emergency, of course. It had only been three hours since my pretzel-eating binge. Who would have thought that five little pretzels could wield such power?

I was taken back to a room and forced to wait until the five little pretzels had been digested. Aargh! I couldn't believe it! A speed bump on top of a speed bump. Another nightmare within a nightmare. I was so ready to be done with cancer.

As I sat on my bed, sulking a little because of the latest turn of events, I was struck with another problem. At first, it was just a tiny itch on the top of my head. I scratched it and felt relief, but a few seconds later it was back. Hmm. Strange. What was going on with my head?

Those tiny itches quickly turned into a major sensation of itchiness that spread from my head, to my neck, and all the way down my back. I tried to scratch the itches, but could not relieve the sensation. It seemed to be multiplying by the second.

The feeling was not a normal itchy feeling, either. No, normally when I had an itch somewhere, I could scratch it and feel relief. With that particular itch, the more I scratched it, the worse it became. It felt as though a thousand ants were crawling along the backside of my body, their little legs tap dancing to a painful beat.

I seized the nurse's call button and pressed it until my thumb started to turn blue. About ten minutes later, just as I was about to scratch the last layer of skin off my back, a nurse appeared.

"I don't know what is going on!" I cried. "I itch all over and it hurts a lot! Is there something you can give me to make it stop?"

As it turns out, I was having an allergic reaction to the IV antibiotics they had administered to me. The nurse gave me a large dose of Benadryl and pretty soon, I was in la-la land with not a care in the world. The itching subsided and the allotted pretzel digestion time had passed. It was time to remove a tissue expander.

Dr. Chen's plan for surgery was to remove the expander, clean out all the infection, and decide if it was safe to put the expander back in. As I drifted into the land of anesthesia, I prayed that my body would cooperate we would be able to stick with that plan.

When I woke up in the recovery room, Dr. Chen was standing next to my bed. Her kind faced was etched with concern. As I tried to clear the cobwebs in my brain, I had the distinct feeling that something must have gone wrong. Why else would she be there in the recovery room?

She explained to me that the surgery went well and that she wanted to be there when I woke up so she could give me a first-hand account of the procedure. She said that there was a lot of infection in my breast. She was confident that she was able to clean it all out, but there was so much bacteria growing on the tissue expander that she was not able to put it back in.

I thought, "*Well, that's okay. You just put a new one in, right?*" Wrong. She continued to explain to me that she could not put a new expander in for fear of there being some bacteria hiding somewhere. It would immediately latch onto the foreign invader (the expander) and then the infection would start all over again.

144

"What we need to do now is wait a week, give you a round of heavy antibiotics to kill any remaining bacteria, and then we can put a new expander in," she concluded.

"Okay, that sounds great. Thanks," I said as I slipped back into my medicated brain fog.

"I woke up to a most unpleasant reality. My right side is gone. My nipple is still there, but it's flat--concave really...I have been completely exhausted today. We didn't get home until 3 A.M. I kept waking up and thinking that this was all a dream. I can't really [be missing an] expander. I can't really be flat. This is just some terrible nightmare that I am going to wake up from...But it's not a dream. It's reality, unfortunately."

The cancer pathway I had traveled on had been very bumpy and uncomfortable up to that point. There were a lot of twists and turns. However, I had been so fortunate! I had been blessed in the fact that once chemo was completed, all my scans had come back clean. All the pathology reports showed clean margins as well, with no trace of the cancer remaining. I was very lucky that my mastectomy had not left me with a concave chest. Instead, I could look down and still see something there. Most women are not that lucky.

But the reality of the situation I now found myself in was like a slap in the face. Now, when I looked down, I could see a normal left side and a non-existent right side. It freaked me out, a lot. You see, when you have had all your breast tissue scraped out of you, the result ends up looking a little different than you might expect.

One would assume (or at least I did) that you would just have a flat chest, when in reality, it was concave. As I scanned the remains of my chest, I thought that it looked like someone had attached a big suction cup to my back and tried to suck my breast out through my back. It was so strange and very disturbing.

As I looked at my disfigured body in the mirror, I received another reality check. I was most definitely still a breast cancer patient. That image would be burned into my mind forever and I feared that it would haunt me for the rest of my life.

During the week that followed, I tried to rest up as much as possible. Thankfully, I was not experiencing a lot of pain, I was just extremely tired, but what else was new?

I also learned a new skill that week--how to stuff your bra. Surprisingly, I did not attempt that in my pre-teen years so it took me a minute to figure out the right way to do it. It took me about three rolls of gauze, bunched up in just the right shape, to fill up the right side of my bra. It was another first to add to the list of firsts that cancer had brought into my life.

Okay. Time for a little checklist. Obnoxious drain removed? Check. Massive breast infection cleaned out? Check. All I had to do now was have a new expander put in and I would be able to move on to radiation and hopefully get closer to the end of my never-ending story.

Twenty-Nine: HEALING

Day 260 of my journey found me back in the hospital, although it was a different hospital than I had previously been to. It was closer to home, which was nice, and the surgical waiting room was more pleasant to be in. I had a brush of sadness as I realized that I had become an expert on hospital waiting rooms and surgical areas.

I arrived at the hospital accompanied by my trusty sidekick, Mark, and we settled in for the wait. We flipped through channels on the TV and tried to make the time fly as quickly as possible.

Finally, around 3 P.M., I took yet another long walk through the halls of a hospital. I was instructed to lie down on yet another cold, hard slab in an operating room. The scenario was becoming all too familiar: the music playing in the background, the bright lights glaring down upon me, the surgical assistants and nurses bustling around me as they gathered tools, chatted with each other, and gave me final instructions. Once again, there was the familiar phrase of, "I'm putting something in your IV now that will make you feel groggy," and then I was out for the count.

~ONE DAY AT A TIME~

I woke up from that surgery and learned that everything went well. No more surprises. A new tissue expander was perfectly placed and filled with enough saline to bring me back to an "A" cup size. I would still be a little lopsided, but at least there would be no more bra stuffing and I was not in concave chest land anymore. Both scenarios brought a smile to my face.

After spending some time in the recovery room, I was once again, driven home by the Love of my Life and just like all the previous drives home from surgeries, I don't remember a thing. In fact, I have no memories of the following day either, but the third day I remember well. It included lots and lots of puking. My body had finally reached its breaking point and was telling me. "No way. No more. I am done."

I am not sure if it was because of the multiple doses of anesthesia that had finally caught up with me, or all the different pain medications I had been on. I suppose it was probably a combination of everything. Whatever it was, it was not good. I could not keep anything down. No liquids. No solids. Nothing. I was sick and oddly enough, it was worse than I had ever felt when going through the nausea battle of chemotherapy.

I called Dr. Chen and begged her to prescribe something to give me some relief. She called in a prescription for a strong anti-nausea medication and a different pain medication. Thankfully, those did the trick and I was finally able to keep some food in my belly and get some rest.

The following day was a Saturday. Everyone was home from school and work and everything was grating on my nerves. My fuse was so short it was practically non-existent.

"I can't wait for [this day] to be over. It's another day to add to the book of failed parenting days. It would be one thing to have to deal with all this cancer crap by myself or even just with Mark. But I still have four kids that I am trying to raise which is no easy task on a good day. It is impossible on a day like day. Satan won today, no doubt about that, and I don't have the energy to fight back.

148

I just want to crawl into a hole and not have to see or talk to anyone--to not have to think about cancer or anything related to it. [I also do not want to think or do anything] that is related to being a parent. I am a failure today. Tomorrow will be better, but for today, I am a failure."

Tempers flared, harsh words were said, and I can't say for sure because I did not write it down anywhere, but I am 90% positive that something was probably thrown either by me, or my cute Abbie. We are frustration throwers and there was a lot of frustration flowing through our house that day. We were all completely done with cancer and all of resentment had bubbled, or rather, exploded to the surface.

Thankfully, the next day was a Sunday. I woke up, determined that I would make that day better than the last. I needed to relish in the feeling that I get when I attend church, partake of the Sacrament, and re-connect with my Savior.

Unfortunately, Sunday mornings were a bit tricky at our home. Mark was gone early for meetings and that left me alone with the kids. Under normal circumstances that would not have been a problem, but I was still feeling twinges of grumpiness and we were running a bit late. I just wanted to get to church on time and forget that the previous week had ever happened.

We had finally found everyone's missing shoes, filled the church bags with the essential snacks, and made our way out to the van. After everyone was situated, I started the van and pulled out of the garage. I immediately sensed that something was wrong.

I thought maybe someone had left a bike out and I was in the process of smashing it to smithereens. I stopped the van, got out, and to my great surprise, saw that the front passenger tire was completely flat. Awesome. Add that to the plate. Throwing in the towel now.

As I stared angrily at the tire, wondering what I was going to do, a car pulled up and my hero emerged. Mark, who rarely comes home between his meetings and the start of church, just happened to think that he needed to come home that Sunday. It was a sign to me that God was still there and that He was aware of my needs.

Mark helped me get van back in the garage and up on a jack. We decided to deal with it after church. We all piled into his car and away we went; a little disheveled, but ready to go to church and renew our spirits.

One thing that I have failed to mention is how much of a role music has played throughout my life, especially during the dark hours of my battle with cancer. As I sat through my church meetings that day, there were two songs that we sang as a congregation that filled my grumpy soul with healing light and again confirmed to me that my Father in Heaven was looking out for me.

One song was "Count Your Blessings."* As I sang the words, I looked around at my children sitting next to me and realized that even with the fatigue, pain, discomfort, flat tires, yelling, grumpiness (need I go on?) -- I had four beautiful and healthy children. Then I looked up at Mark, who was sitting on the stand in front of the congregation, and I felt a flood of gratitude for him. He loved me, even when I was grouchy, grumpy, lopsided, and bald. My gaze then shifted to the people in our congregation. As I looked at them, my thoughts also went to my family and other friends who were not in that congregation. I had been blessed with so many wonderful people in my life. Gratitude filled my heart and the grumpiness started to fade.

The second song was "Cast Thy Burden Upon the Lord."** As we sang that, I truly felt my burden being lifted. My Savior was there with me. He was aware of the struggles that I had been through and the feelings that permeated my soul. He was gently whispering, "Let it go. I've got this. You don't need to carry the burden by yourself."

Going to church that day did exactly what I had hoped it would do. It renewed my broken spirit. It gave me the resolve to let go of the past and move forward. It strengthened my testimony in a loving Savior who knows about my grumpy days, my frustration throwing, and my tendency to yell a little too loudly sometimes. Despite all that, He loves me and is always there for me. He helps me pick up the broken pieces of my life and shows me how I can mend them.

~HEALING~

*"Count Your Blessings." By Johnson Oatman, Jr and Edwin O. Excell. Hymns, 241.

**"Cast Thy Burden Upon the Lord." By Julius Schubring and Felix Mendelssohn. Hymns, 110.

Thirty:

RACE FOR THE CURE

Before I begin this chapter, I need to go back in time to May of 2010. My aunt Cheri had just been diagnosed with cancer and was going through chemotherapy. After visiting her one day, my Aunt Susie and I decided that we were going to sign up for the Race for the Cure, which at that time, was only a few weeks away. I have already alluded to the fact that I don't enjoy running. I wasn't sure how I was going to pull off a 5K, especially considering that it was only weeks away. But Susie and I knew that it was something we needed to do, so I settled into a crash course in running...I mean, jog/walking.

The day of the race was beautiful. I jog/walked until my legs went from being on fire to being completely numb. Despite the loss of feeling in my legs, I finished the entire five kilometers. It was a very moving experience for me and I surprised myself by the scope of emotions that rushed through me while participating in the race. I distinctly remember looking around me before the race had started and thinking that it was amazing how many lives cancer had touched. There were thousands upon thousands of people there and each of them either knew someone with cancer or was a survivor himself or herself. It was incredible.

~RACE FOR THE CURE~

When our portion of the race was complete, we were able to watch the "Survivor's Walk." I stood there, looking at those amazing women, with awestruck tears streaming down my face. Little did I know that just a few short months after that humbling experience, I would be counted among those who have heard the words, "I'm sorry to tell you, but you have cancer."

Fast forward to May 2012. I was standing at the starting line of another Race for the Cure, but this time, I was the one who had been personally touched by cancer. I was the one surrounded by an entire fleet of turquoise shirt-wearing people who were all ready to race in honor of me.

Our team of "Jogging for Jumblies" (Mark's idea for a team name) was bigger than I imagined it would be. A few months earlier, I had put the word out on my blog, and was pleasantly surprised at the amount of people who wanted to participate. They had loved me through it all up to that point and were there to continue to support me amidst the chaos that a Race for the Cure creates: masses of people as far as the eye can see with everyone swimming in a sea of pink shirts, socks, tutus or whatever else can be turned pink. (That's why I chose turquoise for our shirt color and I am so glad that I did. It made it so much easier to spot the people who were in our group. Just a little race tip for ya.)

In the days leading up to the race, I began having second thoughts. When I had signed up for the race, I was on my original "beating cancer plan" and thought that I would be done with radiation and well on my way to recovery. Instead, I was recovering from two unplanned surgeries and had not even crossed the radiation bridge yet. I honestly did not think that I had the strength to walk even one kilometer.

But, I had to do it. My friends and family were there and I knew that I could not let them down, or more importantly, let myself down. At the beginning of my journey, I had promised myself that I would be at that race and by golly; I was going to complete that goal!

We made our way to the starting line, or as close as we could get to it, and waited for the signal to begin "running." The butterflies in my tummy were already starting their race and I was itching to get moving myself.

Finally, we heard the faint sound of the race gun signaling us to start and the sea of pink slowly inched its way forward. We were on our way.

We did not set any records for speed that day, but that did not matter. I relished every step forward because in my mind, it was very symbolic of the way that I had chosen to live my life with cancer: always moving forward, no matter how hard things became.

One of the highlights of the day was being able to participate in the "Survivor's Walk." I was able to be there with my mother-in-law and some of the friends that I had met through my support group. It was the first time that any of us had participated in the Walk. I was so grateful for them, especially my mother-in-law. She was celebrating 16 years as a breast cancer survivor. I look forward to the day when I hit that mark and beyond.

During the walk, I was on such an emotional high that I was so grateful that my sunglasses were on. I didn't want everyone to see the blubbering mess I had become. As I walked with my fellow sisters in cancer, we held our heads high, and none of us could stop the tears. I felt proud to be in the company of so many strong and courageous women.

I searched the crowd for my family and as we turned a corner, I spotted them. When I saw them standing there, all decked out in their Jogging for Jumblies shirts and pink accessories, I completely broke down. All the frustration, anger, and fear from the past nine months hit me right in the heart. Those feelings collided with the sheer joy that I experienced as I marched past my gang. The tears would not stop and neither would the smiling.

I had done it. I did what I set out to do and so much more. I had made it through chemo, surgeries, surprises, sickness, and everything else. One of my favorite moments from that day was captured in a photograph. It was the moment I was able to hug my three little girls. Those sweet, smiling faces, along with the rest of my family, was why I had endured it all and would continue to do whatever else the cancer wanted to throw at me.

When the race and its accompanying festivities were over, we all met back at our house for lots of food and laughter. I was, once again, completely exhausted, but the elation that I felt was immeasurable. It was an incredible weekend and just the boost I needed to send me on my way. I felt my courage strengthened and knew that I could continue on the path, as bumpy as it had become, because I was never going to be alone.

Me and my three lovely ladies at the Race for the Cure
May 2012

Thirty-One: DAY 270

"...Today was Mother's Day and it was a great one. I got spoiled with homemade cards, gifts, and kisses and hugs from my kids. I love these monkeys so much. I am so thankful that my Heavenly Father is allowing me to stay here on earth for a while longer; to work hard and be here to help my children grow and learn. I love being a mom, and one thing that this cancer has given me is a realization of <u>how much</u> I love being a mom and how important it is for me to make sure [that] my kids are a priority in my life. [I need to] love them, be patient with them, spend time with them, and help them...

As hard as this cancer journey has been, it has brought so many good things to my life. It has made me more aware of how I spend my time, how I treat the people around me, what I am doing to strengthen my testimony, and [how] I am [inviting] the Spirit into our lives. I have often said that I hate this cancer, but for these reasons and probably a few more, I love that I have this journey in my life."

Thirty-Two:
GETTING ZAPPED

In the middle of the craziness that the month of May brought into our lives, it also brought the completion of my second round of tissue expander expansion. I had finally reached the point where everything seemed to be where it needed to be. I was not lopsided, there was no more infection lurking about, and my plastic surgeon had given me the thumbs up to start radiation. Hooray! After the agonizing two-month delay, my Radiation Oncologist, Dr. Avizonis, and I agreed that it was time to get the party started.

Step number one in the radiation process involved making a map of my chest and getting some tattoos. That process, like so many others, was a new experience for me. I have never gotten a tattoo before, nor have I ever had a map made of my chest. I can say that I am 100% positive that I hope to not have to experience either of those things again.

I quietly tolerated the tiny pinpricks that pierced my skin, leaving me with six itty-bitty blue dots. Those little blue dots would allow the radiation technicians to line up the linear accelerator (AKA the bug zapping machine) in the exact same spot each time I had a treatment. I ended up with three dots down the center of my chest, one on each side of my rib cage and one where I had the lumpectomy.

With my new tattoos, I was ready to begin the mapping process. It began with some x-rays of my chest. Those x-rays would provide Dr. Avizonis with a clear picture of where the radiation zaps should be directed, thus allowing her to create my personal chest map. (I know that "radiation zap" is not the official medical term, but I like it. It has a nice ring to it, so I am going to go with it.)

Now that I had received my blue baby dots and had more pictures taken of my chest, I was ready to begin radiation. Just kidding. That would have been a little too easy. I would have to go home and wait a few days so that Dr. Avizonis could complete the final map. While I waited, I thought about some of the things that other breast cancer patients had told me about the radiation process. All of them had said that radiation was a piece of cake compared to everything else I had been through. Good. I liked cake. I was ready for a piece of it.

When the day of my appointment arrived, I checked in at the front desk where a kind nurse showed me what my job would be for the next five weeks: check in on the computer, change into a gown, and wait for my turn in the bug zapper. That process of changing and waiting would, by far, be the longest part of my daily radiation appointments.

Once I was in my gown, I flipped through a magazine and tried to keep my mind clear from any nervousness. I practiced some deep breathing exercises until I heard them call out my name. I let out one last big breath and followed the technician down a hallway and into the "vault." It was go time.

As I stepped into the "vault" (which was just a large room with a giant machine in it) I felt as though I had entered one of the rooms in Willy Wonka's chocolate factory; the one where Mike Teavee gets transported into a television set. Everything was white and crisp. The technicians were bustling about, getting everything ready, just like little Oompa Loompas. I chuckled at the thought and wondered if (hoped, really) I might get some chocolate out of the deal.

~GETTING ZAPPED~

One of the technicians instructed me to hop up onto a large, metal slab. Although it was covered with sheets, the coldness of the metal seeped through my thin robe and I knew that I was in for some shivering.

The table I was now lying on was situated directly under the large machine, which looked like a CAT scan machine. It was so large, in fact, it seemed to fill up half the space in the room. The part of the machine that I was most interested in was the arm that would move around me and deliver those precious little "zaps" of radiation. I tried to communicate with it, pleading with it to be kind to my tender skin while it fried my insides.

Now that I was situated on the table, it was time for the fun to begin. First things first, exposing myself to strangers again. Unfortunately, I have lost count of how many people have seen "the girls." The technicians were kind about it though, and they did their best to keep me as covered as possible. Still, we had a few laughs about the situation. Laughter had been, and continued to be the only way to take away the awkwardness of certain situations; such as having strangers poke, prod, and stare at your chest.

Once the table was situated in the right place and the machine was lined up correctly with all my itty-bitty blue dots, the technicians stepped out of the room. My heart pounded wildly in my chest as I heard the massive two-foot thick door slide shut and suddenly I was completely alone, with my chest exposed. The air conditioning kicked in and I focused my concentration on willing my body not to shiver.

The technicians had gone into the room next to my "vault" room. They could see me on a monitor. They could also hear me and talk to me, so I wasn't truly all alone. However, I'm not sure if that made things better or worse in my mind. It all felt too much like I was in a weird science fiction film.

"This session was a little longer than it would normally be because they had to take x-rays first to make sure they aren't radiating anything they don't want to (for example, my lungs and heart.) *I had to lie completely still [for a half an hour] with my arms over my head and my head turned to the left*

159

side. I was okay for the first fifteen minutes, then my arms started falling asleep, my neck started cramping, and my eye started to itch. I survived though...

[During the radiation process, the technicians] move the table I am lying on. [It moves] up and down until my tattoos line up with the right spots on the machine. They [also] have to tape my left breast out of the way so that it doesn't get radiated. (Have you ever had your boob taped down before? Interesting experience for all involved...) *There is a big, round arm on the machine that moves around me and [delivers the radiation zaps.] In between each stage, [the technicians] have to do what is called a 'table kick' where they move the table around a bit to get me in the right position. [The whole radiation procedure] is really pretty fast. I was done in 15 minutes."*

Despite the sleepy arms, the neck cramp, and the itchy eye, I survived the first radiation treatment. It was over before I could even think too much about something going wrong. Once they opened the vault door and un-taped my boob, I jumped off the table and walked quickly to the dressing rooms. This WAS going to be a piece of cake!

I went home feeling like I could truly breathe a sigh of relief. I knew that I would be able to handle the radiation; and handle it I did, over and over again. Twenty-five times to be exact. My life quickly became all about a routine: drive to the hospital--disrobe--put on gown--lie down on cold metal slab--get zapped with the bug zapper--take gown off--put clothes back on--drive home--return tomorrow and repeat the process all over again.

It almost felt <u>too</u> easy. I kept expecting something to go wrong. I suppose I was a little shell-shocked because of the surprise surgeries and never-ending drain situation. It took me a few weeks to accept that the radiation process could actually stick to the plan and not throw me any curve balls.

Day 306: "Today is about the halfway mark for radiation. I am still feeling really good, for the most part. My skin is only slightly red. I am [experiencing] a little more tenderness, especially along my rib cage. But so far, no lymphedema or any major problems...Sometimes I even catch myself NOT thinking about cancer. I can see the light at the end of the tunnel and it's bright!"

Day 312: "I feel so blessed today. I can't believe how well and fast this radiation process is going. I only have eight treatments left and I still have not noticed much redness or change in my skin. I guess it is getting a little more tender to the touch, but to look at it, I don't notice much change at all. I wear my compression sleeve as much as I can stand it to prevent my lymphedema from coming back.

I like to think that Heavenly Father is blessing me with something easy for a moment. I know I can do hard things and I don't mind the challenge. I know those are the times when I learn and grow the most. But it is nice to have this tiny break where things are going smoothly. I hope that the reconstruction surgery will not be too bad.

It is really hard to believe that I am coming up on the year mark of [my] diagnosis. I remember it like it was yesterday; finding the lump...it's been a long year since then, but a good year nonetheless.

I am still here and I plan on being here for a long time. I feel so blessed to be counted among those who have battled cancer and survived.

I hope I will always remember how blessed I am."

Thirty-Three: ESTROGEN. WHO NEEDS IT ANYWAY?

Not this gal, at least not any more. I was thankful to have it when I was ready to welcome children into my family. It definitely came in handy for that process. However, now that it was just a little snack for my cancer, I thought it would be a good idea to be done with it.

I was what you might call a "Fertile Myrtle." I did not have any problems getting pregnant, thankfully. I know so many women who struggle with the pain of infertility and my heart hurts for them. I wish that fertility was something that you could pass on from one person to the next. So many times, I thought, *"Wouldn't it be nice if I could just package up my fertility and pass it on?"*

Despite the wonderful blessing that being so fertile could be, it was also a curse. Because I was Super Estrogen Woman, I was not able to shut it off. For instance, when I was learning about the chemo side effects, the only thing that offered a bit of excitement was when they told me that my periods would stop while I was having the treatments. I had no problem saying goodbye to my old friend

"Aunt Flow." She was a big nuisance and I was looking forward to enjoying a little break from her.

The excitement quickly wore off when two weeks after my first chemotherapy treatment, my period started. It was a very unpleasant and unwelcome surprise. Even my oncologist was a little taken aback.

"That almost never happens," he said.

Well, that's me, the over-achiever; the gal who likes to go the extra mile in everything that she does. If the odds said that I wouldn't have a period during chemo, leave it to my super estrogen powers to plough through and give me one anyway. Fortunately though, that was the one and only period that I had during chemo.

Once all my chemo treatments were over, the guessing game began. Would the temporary menopause I had been experiencing stick around and become full-blown menopause? Or would my super estrogen powers break through and defy the odds yet again?

Super estrogen won again. Only three short months after I finished chemo, "Aunt Flow" returned and she was not happy to have been shoved away like she was. So, she decided to visit twice that month. I was not amused.

My oncologist was recommending a complete hysterectomy. He was of the mindset to get rid of everything that was producing estrogen so that the cancer would be deprived of its favorite meal. I was totally on board with that plan, except for two things: that meant that I would have another surgery before the end of the year and that I would have minimal estrogen being produced in my body. I wasn't sure how exactly how my body would react to that.

I decided it was time to make an appointment with my gynecologist. I had not seen or talked to her since my diagnosis and felt that I needed her expertise to help me make the final decision.

When Dr. Mainwaring walked into the exam room, the first thing she did was wrap me up in a great big hug. She told me that she had been closely monitoring my progress because my other doctors had been sending her all my test results and surgical notes. I felt a huge sense of relief because I had worried that I would not be able to remember everything that I needed to catch her up on.

After the hug and a bit of small talk, we got right down to business. We discussed the issue of me having a lot of estrogen and two ovaries that loved to produce it. That was not good in my situation. Through the course of our discussion, we concluded that yes, a total and complete hysterectomy was the best course of action for me.

That decision was solidified in my mind during the physical exam that took place just a few moments after our discussion. While Dr. Mainwaring was checking my ovaries, she felt a cyst on my right one. She scheduled me for an ultrasound so that we could have it checked out right away. *"Please"*, I thought, *"not again! I can't go on this roller coaster ride again."* I tried to focus on the rest of our conversation and quell the giant knot that was forming in my stomach.

> *"I hate to even say that I am not worried about it. Look where [I] ended up last time I wasn't worried about a lump. But really, the odds of it being cancerous are pretty low. I had chemo running through my body for four months and [the cyst] was not picked up in two different PET scans. I guess there is always a possibility, especially considering the fact that the cancer was in my lymph nodes and that it needs estrogen to grow. My ovaries love to produce estrogen so it would be [the] perfect place [to camp out.] Of course I am a little on the paranoid side--with good reason--but I have to remember to have faith and not fear."*

As the cancer bells silently screamed in my head, Dr. Mainwaring and I concluded my appointment by discussing the pros and cons of having a hysterectomy at 34 years of age.

The cons: I would go directly into menopause which would include hot flashes, vaginal dryness, bone loss, weight gain, and possibly, heart issues. The good news was that some of those symptoms had the potential of only lasting for 5-10 years. Although I would always have to be mindful of my bones and

164

cardiovascular system. I would also have to be diligent about exercising so that I could keep my body as healthy as possible.

The pros: Very little estrogen left to grow cancer, which outweighed all the cons by a long shot.

I would like to order one hysterectomy, please.

Thirty-Four:

ANOTHER PHASE COMPLETE

*D*ay 321: *"Well, I think everything is okay. I had the ultrasound yesterday morning. The technician was very sweet and said, 'We didn't have this conversation and I am not a doctor, but this looks like it is just a cyst.' She said that she [would] follow up and make sure that Dr. Mainwaring got the results as soon as possible. I haven't heard anything yet, so I am assuming that no news is good news. I was a little [sore and] tender yesterday after the ultrasound, but it hasn't really bothered me today.*

The thing that is starting to bother me, unfortunately, is my radiated skin. I am finally [experiencing] the discomfort that I was not looking forward to. It started on Sunday. I noticed that my clavicle area hurt. It was hurting because my shirt was rubbing against it. Sure enough, my skin is pretty raw there.

My [right] nipple is also having some issues. I am glad that I [don't have any] feeling there anymore because it looks very sore. I am also really red and sore under my arm. I got some special bandages from the nurses yesterday and they have helped a lot. It's kind of like a sticky piece of thin foam. It just sticks to my skin and cushions it so my clothes don't rub on it. But the great news is, I only have one treatment left...one more check on the checklist. It's hard to believe I am really to this point. When I look back on the whole process, I feel like it has gone by so fast. But I remember [going through bad moments] and feeling like [they] were never going to end.

I will be really glad when I can have my reconstruction and get these tissue expanders out. Every morning seems to be a bit worse. I am just sore and that's no fun, but I am here and able to complain about it, so that is good!"

*Day 324: "Hooray! No more radiation! It feels so good to be able to complete one more part of the process. I wish I could go right in and have these tissue expanders taken out. They usually don't bother me during the day, but [every morning] when I wake up, [I am so] sore. They even woke me up last night because they were hurting. *Sigh.* Just a little longer."*

Day 327: "Well, they say it always gets worse before it gets better. That's definitely true. It has been true with chemo, my surgeries, and now it rings true with my radiation burns. They have now entered a phase where they itch like crazy, but it hurts when I try to scratch the itch. The last two nights I have just laid in bed without a shirt on because my shirts rub against the burns. Hopefully [the burns] will start feeling better in the next day or two."

Day 329: "I find it hard to adjust to my 'normal' life now. I have spent the last 11 months practically sleeping, eating, and breathing cancer. Now that I don't have to think about it anymore, it's very weird. I still have my surgeries to look forward to, but I am cancer free. I don't have to think about cancer anymore. That is a wonderful feeling, but it's going to take some time to get used to..."

Standing in front of the linear accelerator machine
July 2012

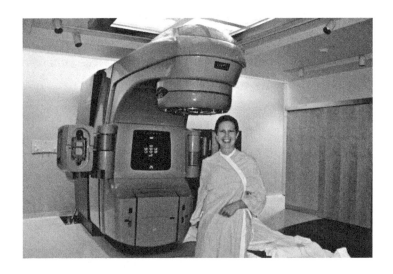

Thirty-Five: MY
"LIFE AFTER CANCER"
PHASE BEGINS

As my time with radiation ended and I received the great news that the cyst on my ovary was nothing to be concerned about, I began a new phase in my journey; the "life after cancer" phase. For months now I had done nothing but try to survive. I had pushed myself to the limit and beyond. Now it was time to see what life would be like on the other side of cancer.

My radiation burns were fading. Most of the dead skin had peeled away leaving soft, pink, fresh looking skin in its place. My lymphedema was behaving for the moment and the tightness of the skin on the right side of my body was slowly loosening. With each passing day, I was able to lift my arm just a little bit higher.

Something that I had not expected in the "life after cancer" phase, however, was how much I would still be suffering from the side effects of chemo. One would assume that once you are done having poison injected into your body, you return to normal, right? Wrong. Let us not forget the word *poison*. I had poison injected into my body to kill another poison that was trying to kill me. The chemo did its job of killing the cancer, but the other things that it had killed in its wake of destruction left me wondering if I would ever be able to feel like myself again.

There were the standard side effects of hair loss and nausea, of course, and fortunately, those ended once I had completed all my chemo treatments. My hair was coming in nicely and my head was starting to fill up with lots of soft, little curls. I had never had naturally curly hair before so that was a new adventure, but it was a welcome one. I really loved my little curly locks and even though the texture was different (it felt a lot like a baby's fine hair), I was so grateful to have hair again.

Another side effect that I was battling was neuropathy. It would hit me out of nowhere causing waves of pain in my feet. Fortunately, the pain subsided quickly, but it left my feet numb for a few minutes afterward. It was an interesting experience to walk on numb feet, especially when I was wearing high heels.

Along with the lingering side effects from the chemotherapy, I was also experiencing some residual effects from my breast surgeries. During the surgeries, a lot of nerves had been severed. That left my breasts mostly numb with basically zero hope of the feeling ever coming back. Some of those nerves did not like being separated and occasionally, I would feel a little jolt of searing pain as those nerves tried to reconnect with each other. After the pain of that re-connection attempt, I would experience what I have termed, "boob itch", a most unpleasant sensation. It was a horrible itch that started deep in my breast and no matter how hard I tried, I just could not scratch it. It drove me completely bonkers (and still does on occasion).

I tried to be discreet when the "boob itch" would strike and not have it look like I was trying to claw my breast off. But I am sure that people have caught me in a bad itch moment and have wondered why I was wrestling with my chest.

Another thing I was battling was the loss of a comfortable sleeping position. I have always been a stomach sleeper and now, thanks to the evil tissue expanders, healing scars, and everything else, I had to try to find another

170

comfortable position that would allow me to get the rest I needed. It wasn't working out so well. I felt like instead of sleeping, I just tossed and turned most of the night. I desperately wanted to be rid of those pesky tissue expanders so that I could (hopefully) resume my normal sleeping position and get the sleep that my body needed to rejuvenate and heal.

That loss of sleep contributed heavily to the next side effect on my list: fatigue. I was experiencing an amount of fatigue like I had never known before. It was a tiredness that seeped deep into my bones. After almost a year of being beaten down, my poor body was just completely worn out. I felt like it had aged about 40 years. My stamina was nearly non-existent. I huffed and puffed just walking up a set of stairs. I was slowly trying to work my way into a good exercise routine, but it wasn't going very well.

There were days when I would feel pretty good and I tried to use my small bursts of energy wisely. It became a strange game of trying to figure out how to not overdo it and conserve some of my precious energy for the next day. It was exhausting trying to not be exhausted.

I was doing my best to try and manage all the lingering side effects, but the one that was the hardest for me to adjust to would have to be the "chemo brain." (Chemo brain is an actual diagnosis that many post-cancer patients have to learn to live with. It can happen anytime during and after chemotherapy treatments and can be immensely frustrating.)

Before cancer, I struggled with "mom brain." Did you know that having kids actually kills brain cells? *It's true!* Or at least, it <u>feels</u> like it's true. My four pregnancies and the process of raising my little angels had already robbed me of precious brain function. Now add to that the effects of the chemo brain, and you have a complete disaster.

My mantra became "If I only had a brain," just like the scarecrow from the *Wizard of Oz*. *If I only had a brain* I would be able to remember what I was supposed to be doing from one minute to the next. *If I only had a brain* I would not have to write down every, single, little thing that someone asked me to do because if I didn't write it down, it would be gone. Out of my brain. As if the conversation never happened. *If I only had a brain* I would not wander around the house knowing that I was looking for something, but not having the slightest clue of what I was searching for.

In my life before cancer, I had been fairly efficient at multi-tasking. Now, even the simplest of tasks required my complete, undivided attention. Gone were the days of making dinner while working on bills and other items at the computer. It I wanted dinner to be cooked, and cooked well, I needed to give it my full attention. (Which, in all honesty, is probably the better way to go anyway. It was one of the important lessons that I learned...SLOW DOWN! Stop trying to do so many things at once! Pay attention to the things that really matter and stop trying to be Superwoman all the time.)

As the year mark of my diagnosis approached, I started to experience a plethora of emotions on top of dealing with all the physical side effects. One minute I felt excitement. *Yes! I have made it one year!* The next minute I would feel anxiety about what memories would be stirred up as I hit each milestone: one year from the start of chemo, one year from the end of chemo, one year from my surgeries. You get the picture.

I still could not walk into the cancer center without being assaulted by the smell that hit my nostrils. As soon as the sliding glass doors opened, my stomach started churning. I wish I had the words to accurately describe the smell. It was a combination of a sterile environment, bandages, and medication all jumbled up into one nauseating aroma. I hoped that with time, I would be able to go there without having my mind associate the smell with feeling sick. After all, time heals all wounds, right?

Thirty-Six: 8-19-12

"A year after [my] first entry and I am writing this as a free woman. I wish I could say that I am completely done with the journey, but I am not quite there yet. [I still have] two surgeries to go and medication to take for the next five years, but just knowing that chemo, radiation, and the other hard parts are behind me is a beautiful thing.

I mentioned on my blog that now it is time for me to get back on track, but it's a different track than I was on. The one I was on before was definitely a racetrack. I was just running and running without taking time to rest and rebuild. This track that I am on now (and hopefully will stay on for a while) is a much more leisurely-paced track. I am sure I will have my bursts of speed here and there, but I plan to mostly stay at an easy jog. I am striving to do more of the better and best things this life has to offer-- not just the good. Things like: spending quality time with my family, studying the scriptures, going to the temple, seeking for opportunities to serve others, and teaching my kids how to serve.

I have made it through a year of [a great] battle. I have a lot of battle wounds, but they are healing. I will always have the scars to remind me of the lessons I have learned. I wear those scars with pride, the visible ones, and the ones on my soul.

I am still standing. I am still living. I am eternally thankful to a loving Father in Heaven who has mercifully granted me more time on earth. It is my hope and prayer that I do not waste that precious time; that I may use it to do His will and spread His love.

I don't know how often I will write in this particular journal now. My initial year with cancer has come to a close. Thank you, pretty pink journal, for being a way for me to record this small journey in my life; the happy moments, the sad moments, and everything in between."

Thirty-Seven:
RECONSTRUCTION:
PART TWO

In the months between my first cancer anniversary and my second reconstruction surgery, life continued to cruise along. My days were filled with the busyness of being a mother, a teacher, a wife, and a cancer survivor.

It was nice to be busy and have the distraction from my aching body. Some days I found myself not even thinking about cancer. Nonetheless, there wasn't anything that could take my mind off the tissue expanders and as my surgery date crept closer, I found myself growing more and more impatient. I could not wait to get rid of those torture devices.

They made my breasts hurt from the inside out. I don't even know if that can make sense unless you have experienced it. I felt as though I had two giant boulders sitting in my chest, pressing tightly against my skin and muscles. The tightness was agonizing and there were many days that I felt as though my skin were screaming for mercy.

Because of the tightness and pain, it made for some awkward hugs. It also made it difficult to snuggle with my little munchkins. One day, Ellie plopped down next to me on the couch and her head hit against my chest. She sat up, rubbed the back of her head and said, "Ouch, Mommy! That hurt!" I'm sorry babe. I didn't mean to give you a concussion with my chest rocks.

I dreamed of the day that my plastic surgeon would gently remove the boulders and replace them with soft, silicone implants. I was excited to see the magic she would work and what the finished products would look like. I knew that they would never be the same as the originals and that made me a little sad. Even though they had tried to kill me, I still missed them and although the new set would help me feel and look "normal", the truth of the matter was, they would still be different.

The day of my reconstruction finally came and something about the date made me feel like it could be my lucky day. 10-11-12. Good things had to happen on a date like that!

"...I had my reconstruction surgery today. Hooray! No more tissue expanders for me! I am a little out of it still...I will write more about the surgery later. I just wanted to write today since the date is so cool..."

"...It is so weird to feel like I was asleep for only two seconds when the surgery actually took about two hours. I hardly remember anything. I don't remember going to the recovery room at all. I vaguely remember a nurse talking to me.

We stopped by Target [on the way home so that Mark could] pick up my medication. Then we stopped to grab some lunch. The rest of the afternoon I have been in and out of consciousness. I have also been EXTREMELY grumpy and irritable. I hate feeling this way. Hopefully tomorrow will be better."

Sadly, tomorrow was not better, neither was the following day. I wasn't sure why I was so grumpy. My surgery went well and I had not experienced any complications. The evil tissue expanders were gone and I did not have to stay in the hospital overnight. I should have been so happy!

Unfortunately, somewhere between the hospital and home, my evil twin had traded places with me and was creating some very negative situations. She was allowing everyone and everything to agitate me. In hindsight, I realized that I should have just barricaded myself in my room, but at the time, I just couldn't do it.

I couldn't understand why I was so irritable. I had so many people being kind to me. Friends and neighbors were bringing us dinners and taking our kids out to have some fun. My husband was so helpful and willing to do anything that I asked of him. My phone was jumping around like a jackrabbit as it received text messages from many lovely family members and friends. I was being lifted up with so much love that I should have been happy, but I was not.

Although I had plenty of reasons to be happy, I had just as many reasons to be grumpy: too much anesthesia, poison, pain medication, and general discomfort over the last year and a half of my life had built up and it just became too overwhelming. Unfortunately, I let the irritability take over and my family, whom I had fought so hard for, was taking the brunt of my unkindness. They did not deserve it, but I could not stop the madness.

One of the things that added to my anger was when I stepped out of the shower and was able to see my chest for the very first time since surgery. I had naively thought that once the bandages came off, everything would look perfect. What I saw was nothing like I had pictured in my mind.

As I stood in front of the mirror, looking at my bruised and battered breasts, I lost it. I let the anger completely take over and there was no turning back. I was mad at the wretched cancer that took away over a year of my life. I was mad that I had to be in pain and uncomfortable which was causing me to be grumpy with my little family. I was mad that I had to live with this "new set" which was nothing like the "old set" and I wanted that "old set" back.

I was also mad that I had short hair when all I wanted was to be able to feel my long hair against my back. I wanted to pull it up in a messy bun. I wanted to have Mark be able to run his fingers through it and play with it while we watched television.

I would love to be able to write that after foaming at the mouth and raging like a lunatic, I was able to feel peace, calm, and serenity. Nope. The peace did not come because I wouldn't let it. A war of epic proportions was seething inside me and for the moment, I was caught up in the whirlwind of negativity.

Sunday morning dawned and with it came three sweet, smiling (and somewhat toothless) faces. As I tried to shake off sleep, I saw that my cute girlies were carrying a tray of interesting looking food. I was instantly contrite. For the past three days, I had said mean things to them. I had also exhibited very little patience and yet, here they were, bringing me breakfast in bed.

I looked over the tray they had placed before me. There were two slices of warmish cinnamon toast, a bowl full of what I assumed was an apple that had been chopped up beyond recognition, the salt and pepper shakers, a glass of water, and a homemade caramel. Alongside the food was a precious handmade card that read, *"We love mom. An apple a day keeps the doctor away!"* It was the perfect breakfast to cure an overly grumpy mommy.

Bless those cute little angels! I did not deserve the goodness that they shared. I had not been nice at all, but they forgave me. They got over the fact that I had been screaming at them for three days straight. They didn't care what my hair or chest looked like or if I was grumpy, or ornery, or sad. All they knew was that their mommy was still with them and even though she had been horrible to them, they knew that she still loved them.

Cancer had taken away a lot of things, but that's just it; they were only "things." It could not take away our love for each other. As I came to that realization and thought about my angel girls, I felt the darkness leave and a sweet, peaceful feeling came back into our home.

_____

~RECONSTRUCTION: PART TWO~

Day 428: "Well, ten days have gone by since my surgery. I am feeling much better about everything. The swelling has gone down and I am pretty pleased with how everything looks. I met with Dr. Chen on Friday and it looks like I will probably have to [have surgery] at least one more time. There are a couple of places where I can see the outline of the implant. [I can also] feel it when I rub my hand over it. I knew it was a risk and that we would probably have to go back and have her place Alloderm in those spots. Alloderm is cadaver tissue. It will cushion the implant. Right now, because I have no breast tissue, it is just the implant, a thin ridge of muscle, and then my skin...So long term, it will be better to get the Alloderm so that the implant doesn't [end up] irritating my skin.

I also saw Dr. Chandramouli yesterday. I am still on the [every] three-month visit plan with him. My white blood count is a little low, but that's normal. It also explains why I am little sluggish; that and I just had surgery. But other than those things, everything else looks good."

Thirty-Eight: DAY 450

Day 450: "Man, one thing that continues to surprise me is just how tired I am. I feel it in my whole body--just a tiredness to my bones, literally. By the end of each day, I am spent. My legs hurt and I feel like an old lady when I try to get up.

For the most part, I feel like I have adjusted to the new, normal way of life. I am learning how to balance my time wisely and not do too much in one day. I am not perfect, of course, and some days I push too hard and overdo it.

I have learned many lessons over the past 450 days. Patience is a running theme in my life--always has been, always will be. There is one lesson though, that I really hope I can remember in the coming months and years as I move on to other phases in my life. That is to remember just how important life is, how lucky I am to be alive and to be a wife and a mother, and how I need to fill my life with the best things, not just the good things. My time with my kids is precious and short. They are getting bigger every day. My plan is to just enjoy and savor every moment I have with them [from here on out.]

The scriptures have always been important in my life, but I am not a great scriptorian. I have always had a hard time settling down and really reading and studying them. I have had the impression a few times now, that I need to prepare my mind in spiritual matters, so I have tried really hard to make my scripture study time more productive.

It's a little easier now with all the kids in school. I have quite a few hours of quiet time during the day and I have taken advantage of it. I have had to let other things go. They were still good things, but now is the time to focus on the best things; the things that my Savior needs me to do: temple worship, time in the scriptures, time with my family, and serving others.

In about another month, I will be in the hospital again having yet another surgery. I am really not looking forward to the recovery of this one--my hysterectomy. It is going to be painful. I am, however, looking forward to no more periods and hopefully, no more 'crazy mom' moments because of whacked out hormones. I know there is going to be lots of adjusting as my body can never have estrogen again, but it seems like I am nicer without estrogen anyway.

I will also be happy to not have any estrogen so I can put my mind at ease. I know as long as there is estrogen in my body, I have the risk of the cancer coming back. So even though the recovery is going to be miserable, it will be worth it for my peace of mind."

Thirty-Nine:

LEAVING ESTROGEN

IN THE DUST

December 12, 2012: 12-12-12; the day of my hysterectomy. I felt as though the uniqueness of the date would bring me luck, just as it had on the day of my reconstruction surgery.

With the hysterectomy, I was taking another giant step forward in being able to push thoughts of cancer out of my mind. I was not looking forward to another surgery, another bout with anesthesia, and another six weeks (at least) of taking it easy. I was, however, looking forward to no more periods.

I also experienced feelings of excitement when I allowed myself to think that the surgery was part of the end of my journey. But that excitement was short-lived. Too many times I had the thought that I had reached an ending, when it really turned out to be another beginning. What beginning would the hysterectomy create or could it actually be part of an ending?

As I pondered that question, I began to change my thought process about the whole experience. Instead of saying that I was "closing the book on cancer", I realized that my book of cancer was not a book at all, but rather a portion in the book of my life. The chapters on cancer were long and had proved to be very difficult to get through, but somehow, I was managing. I concluded that now it was just time to dive into another chapter, which would be followed by another, and another, for the rest of my life.

My hysterectomy chapter began on that bitter cold December 12th morning. The plan was for Dr. Mainwaring to perform a complete hysterectomy, along with some repairs to my bladder. The surgery took a little over three hours and everything went well.

As I struggled to fight my way out of the anesthesia fog, I quickly realized that I was in for something not good. All I could feel was intense pain. In my previous surgeries, I had small amounts of pain that were completely manageable. Now, however, I felt pulsating waves of deep, intense pain and they were not about to be shut down by pain meds.

I writhed about on the bed, clutching my abdomen while moaning and begging for pain medication. When the nurse gave me a dose of Demerol, I felt instant relief from the pain, but I also had to scramble to find the kidney-shaped plastic barf tray. It was truly one of the less than glamorous times in my life and once again, the Love of my Life had to witness all the grotesqueness.

"I was able to go home on Thursday afternoon, and I have been pretty much laid up since then. The first few days were a bit rough, pain wise. I felt like I was having really bad menstrual cramps. The night [that I had spent] in the hospital was one of the longest nights of my life. I had a catheter in [along with] a bunch of cotton packing. (The cotton packing was to help with the bleeding.)

I could not get comfortable. Once the nurses took out the catheter and cotton packing, [I felt] a huge [amount of] relief. I can't believe how much packing they pulled out of me. It had to have been like three or four feet!

...I have discovered that my body will no longer tolerate any pain meds stronger than Ibuprofen and Tylenol. [If I take anything stronger,] I start hallucinating and feel like people are watching me. I [also] feel like I can't move or talk. It's a scary feeling."

It took me a good six weeks to feel like I could move around at a pace faster than turtle speed. Part of the problem was that I had a couple of little hiccups during the recovery period. Those issues set me back a bit. Of course! Leave it to me, the "extra-miler!" I insist on going the extra mile in everything that I do-- including recovering from major surgery.

Day 514: "When I started this journal, there was not even one part of me that thought I would still be writing at day 514. I have now been at this battle for over 500 days and I AM EXHAUSTED!!

I just met with Dr. Chen and found out that I will indeed be going back to the surgery table at least one more time, possibly two. My breasts are sagging a bit. We are not really sure why. Possibly the implants are too heavy. So, in May, [I will have another surgery] so Dr. Chen can use Alloderm to strengthen the underside [of my breasts.]

Hopefully I will be able to [keep the size that I am now], but more than likely I will have to go down a size. [Dr. Chen] is also going to have to use the Alloderm to fill in a few spots where my skin looks too thin, but [that may have to be] a separate surgery.

I am tired of 'looking forward' to another surgery. I am tired of making my sweet husband wait in the wings while I go under the knife. I am tired of making lists of things that I hope to be able to do when I feel up to it. Blah...cancer is dumb.

Physically, I am feeling okay. I was having more pain last week so I called Dr. Mainwaring and she checked everything out.

I didn't have an infection, which is good, but I do have a couple of places where some scar tissue is building up...that is what is causing the [increase of] pain.

It was getting to the point where I couldn't sit very well. So [Dr. Mainwaring] poked and prodded for a bit (which felt just wonderful--said with A LOT of sarcasm) and she was able to loosen things up. After a few days of Ibuprofen, I feel a lot better.

My hair, on the other hand, is not a good thing. I am tolerating it for the moment. I've had a few bad days of comb throwing and stomping my feet because I really just hate the style I have right now.

I am glad to have the hair back [and] I knew that I was going to have to go through an awkward stage or two. [But now that I am in that awkward stage] I hope it won't have to last very long. Please grow fast little hairs."

Day 532: "Today is a big milestone. It marks one year since my last chemo treatment. It's really hard to believe that it has been a year since that wonderful day. We had the pink party with so many family and friends...I feel truly blessed.

So how do I feel one year after chemo? TIRED! Fatigue is now a part of my daily life. Part of that fatigue is [because] of all the surgeries and everything [as well.] The good news is, now that I can start exercising again, I hope that I will be able to get some energy and stamina back.

I have pretty much recovered from my hysterectomy. I had my six-week check up on Tuesday and [Dr. Mainwaring] had to fix another spot where the scar tissue was growing in weird. That was unpleasant. [After the experience,] I went home and put myself to bed.

But I felt pretty normal the next day and have felt good since. I am also feeling a little better about my hair. Julie colored it a couple of days ago and we trimmed up the back quite a bit. It looks much better now and I am learning new tricks every day. [I just have to take things] one day at a time. That's all I can do."

Forty: THE OTHER SIDE OF THE MOUNTAIN

"How are you feeling?"

That was the million-dollar question. As in, if I had a nickel for every time someone asked me that, I would be a millionaire. Please don't get me wrong. I honestly appreciated everyone's concern for my well being and I was spoiled with attention during the whole cancer journey. I will always be grateful to each person who expressed their love and support through words and actions.

It was just hard to hear that question because each time it was asked of me, I was reminded that I was still struggling. I didn't want to be struggling anymore. I wanted to feel better than I felt, physically and mentally.

Of course, my usual response to that question was, "I feel great! Except for the fact that I am tired all the time, things are going well." It was an honest answer, but just saying the word "tired" did not even come close to being able to express how I was feeling.

I can say with certainty that I had never felt that tired in all my life. Not even when I was pregnant or when I was a new parent living on just a few hours of sleep each night. There was no other tired feeling to compare it to. I was tired in my bones. Tired in my muscles. Tired in my brain.

Most days I was able to push through all the discomforts that continued to plague me such as: hot flashes, chemo brain, achy joints and bones, etc. Most of the time I just felt so blessed to have a second chance at life, that I could overlook all the discomfort. But there were days when a fresh wave of fatigue would slam me to the ground and I had no choice but to shut down--physically and mentally. I hated those days.

It was during that time in my after-cancer life when I had a real "Ah-ha" moment; I was not the only one who was fighting a daily battle of survival. Everyone in the world has times in their lives when they experience a "cancer" of sorts--something that robs them of time and health or something that is just plain hard to muddle through. When those "cancers" come, we really have two choices: We can either succumb to the "cancer" and let it over-run our lives, or we can fight it. My choice was, and still is, to fight.

As I continued to blog about my thoughts and feelings, I noticed that I seemed to be entering new territory. The blogs that I followed which were written by other cancer survivors seemed to stop being updated once the survivor's active treatment schedule concluded. My guess was that they were feeling the same tiredness I was and it made it too difficult to continue.

Because I felt that my cancer journey was far from over, I forced myself to keep writing. I could not stop writing in my pink journal and I could not allow myself to stop sharing my journey on my blog. I felt like I needed to let people (especially other cancer survivors) know what the other side of the mountain looked like.

I was determined to keep moving forward. Some days it felt like I was using every ounce of strength within me to wrench free from the suffocating grip of the cancer quicksand. Those were the times that I had to focus intently on the top of the mountain. By drawing my attention there, I could keep moving upward.

When I felt like I had finally reached the topmost part of my mountain, the view took me completely off guard. It looked nothing like I had imagined it would. I did not find a beautiful, flat meadow with rippling blades of grass swaying in the breeze. Instead, there was something even more breathtaking. It was another mountain, towering before me with majestic peaks and awe-inspiring valleys; beckoning me to explore every crack and crevice.

As I faced this new majestic wonder, I knew that I could face it as a seasoned climber. I had scaled a mountain that I never thought I would be able to. That climb had left me empowered with the knowledge and courage that I needed to ascend anything that would ever be placed before me because I knew that I could, can, and will always be able to do hard things.

Forty-One: DAY 673

"This will officially be my last entry in this little pink journal of mine. It has almost been two years since I started writing in it. It's hard to believe it has been that long. It still feels like yesterday [that] I was shocked to the core with the news. I have been through so much. Sometimes it feels very much like a dream.

I am thankful for the inspiration I had to keep a journal of the experience. It will always be a wonderful thing to look back on and to pass down through the generations.

It is wonderful to say that I am officially D-O-N-E. I had my last surgery on May 31, 2013. I love my plastic surgeon. She is a true miracle worker and I feel so blessed to have been sent her direction. If I didn't have a few dozen scars, you would never know that anything had happened to these "girls" of mine. I am so fortunate to have them look as good as they do. I know it could be a lot worse.

I went to Carol's Mastectomy Boutique about a week ago to get fitted for a good, supportive bra. While I was there, I read a newspaper article about one of the owners. She was diagnosed [with breast cancer] at the age of 27.

In the article, there was a quote from her husband. He said, 'Every time I look at that scar, I am reminded that God could have taken you. Instead, he chose to take your breasts so that you could stay here and teach the boys about Jesus.' It really struck a chord with me.

I was facing death. It was a real possibility. But for whatever reason, the Lord needs me to continue my work here on earth. I do believe one of those reasons is to continue raising my kids and teaching them about Jesus. I have to remind myself of that on a daily basis because I get wrapped up in silly things and get distracted from what I really need to be doing.

Back to my surgery...I went to a new surgical center and I hope to never have to go back [there.] It was an older facility. Everyone was nice enough and they actually had a heated operating table, which I enjoyed for about a minute before I drifted off into la-la land. [The problem came in recovery.]

When I woke up, my right arm was completely numb, and it was bothering me. In my altered state of consciousness, I remember one of the nurses saying that they had put the blood pressure cuff on it for a little bit. It I hadn't been so out of it, I would have complained very loudly about that. I had it written in big, black letters on my arm: 'NO BP or IV' (Having blood pressure taken or an IV placed on my right arm increased my risk for the lymphedema to flare up.) *By the time I got home, my arm was already swelling and so were my hand and fingers. They were still numb, but starting to tingle a bit. I was not a happy camper about the situation.*

After a day or so, the numbness went away, but I had to wear my compression sleeve for about a week to keep it down. The surgery itself went really well though. [Dr. Chen] was originally planning on going down an implant size, but she was able to reinforce [the area well enough] with Alloderm tissue [that she was able to keep my original implant size.] That made me happy.

It was a bit of a shocker when I went to take a shower for the first time. I had about 30 little 'packets' stitched all over my breasts. [My chest] looked like a tied quilt. The stitches were holding the Alloderm in place. It looked crazy. Add my two drains to that and I was looking pretty sexy. I [also] had a big piece of sticky plastic wrap over my whole chest to keep the germs away.

I was able to get the drains out about a week after surgery. That was a heavenly day. They are so uncomfortable. I had to sleep sitting up for a whole week. Not fun. About ten days after surgery, I was able to go in and have all of the sutures taken out. That was heavenly too because they were SUPER itchy...

I still have to wear an ace bandage [wrapped] tightly around the bottom of my breasts to help hold them up while everything heals.

I am not supposed to lift anything over ten pounds either. I need to be better about that. It is a really hard thing to do, but I don't want to mess anything up. I am so beyond being done with this chapter of my life.

I really feel a sense of completion with this surgery. I know there is not another one coming so I feel I can finally start moving forward for good. It's a good thing too, because I am out of pages in this book.

Thank you, little pink journal, for being such a good companion on this long and windy road. I look forward to reading your pages and using them as a reminder of how precious life is and how much my Heavenly Father loves me."

PART TWO

Forty-Two:

A DIFFERENT ENDING

Ending. "A final part of something, especially a period of time." (According to *Merriam-Webster* anyway.) If that is the case, I had definitely hit an ending. All the treatments that had been recommended were complete. I could now look forward to moving on with my life and setting cancer on a shelf high above me, never to be reached for again. Unfortunately, I overlooked one thing: Cancer does not like to be put on a shelf.

Once it latches onto you, it is there to stay, even if it is not actively ravaging your body anymore. It sits in the dark recesses of your brain and taunts you. It waits for you to get comfortable and then it sends out its tentacles, twisting and winding around you until you can no longer move.

In the beginning, I just wanted to get the surgeries and treatments over with as quickly as possible so that I could move on with my life and pretend that the whole thing had never happened. I naively thought that it would be like having the flu--you have it, you would be miserable for a while, and then you would move on.

~A DIFFERENT ENDING~

Now that I was in the aftermath of cancer, I was surprised to find out that I still had a very large battle to fight. That battle came in the form of PTSD, or Post Traumatic Stress Disorder. PTSD is a disorder associated with anxiety. It can occur after a period of major trauma in your life, usually one involving injury or the possibility of death.

Let's see, had I experienced any periods of trauma, injury, or the possibility of death? The answer to that would be a big, fat YES! The diagnosis, active treatments, and surgeries alone were reason enough for me to be struggling with PTSD. But what contributed the most were some events that shook my emotional state and brought me to my knees in more ways than one.

While writing this book, I launched a great debate in my mind. Do I include my experience with PTSD or not? It has proven to be the hardest part to write about. I have grappled with how to introduce it, organize it, write about it, and make it work.

There has been much rearranging and backspacing of words, along with the occasional outburst of "Why am I doing this?" I don't know why it has been such a struggle. I only know that it needs to be included because it will help me achieve one of my goals for this book: inspiring others who are in the trenches of fighting cancer. I have found that not a lot of people talk about what happens in the aftershock of cancer and it is a story that I feel needs to be shared.

Forty-Three:
HEARTACHE & HEALING

The series of events leading up to my PTSD diagnosis began shortly before my last reconstruction surgery. At that point in time, I had finally been able to push cancer to the very back of my mind. The active treatments were over, my surgeries were almost complete, and I was feeling stronger every day. Then cancer did something unforgivable. It messed with my Superman.

My grandpa was a real "man's man." He exuded masculinity, and I believe he had conquered the vast majority of the wilderness in our great state. Whether on purpose or on accident, he had seen a lot of amazing places. He was an explorer in every sense of the word.

He also seemed indestructible to me. I can't tell you how many times I would go visit with my grandparents only to find that my grandpa was bleeding somewhere. I would draw his attention to the injury and he would just shrug it off.

"Oh that?" he replied. "It's nothing. Just a little scratch."

In my mind, there was nothing that could hurt him, so when he was diagnosed with AML (Acute Myeloid Leukemia) I figured that it would be just another bleeding wound that he would shrug off.

Day 632: "I thought I should write an update. I was debating on whether or not to include the day count on this entry. I decided to do it, because as much as I hate to admit it, cancer is still a part of my everyday life. I hope to reach the point where I don't feel like it is.

Unfortunately, I don't think I will ever be able to escape cancer for good. It will continue to touch my life, even when I am not the one fighting it. We found out ten days ago that my sweet Grandpa Fowlks has AML. Cancer. Originally the doctor gave him two months to live. Last Monday, I had the privilege of accompanying him and my grandma as they met with another doctor. [She was able to give us] a small sliver of hope.

Because of his general good health (he was 78 years old and walking 6 miles a day) *he has started a mild form of chemotherapy [that will] hopefully slow things down and give us a little more time with him. How much time is hard to say. This past week he has gone up to the hospital every day to have poison run through his veins.*

My heart has been completely broken. I can't believe that this is happening to my Superman grandpa. I think he is handling things well, for the most part. He definitely would like to hang around here longer, but he is not afraid to die and looks forward to seeing his family and friends on the other side...

I went up to the hospital on Friday [so that I could] sit with [my grandparents] during the chemo infusion. It is hard to see my grandpa look so tired. Sitting there [also] brought back memories of my own time with chemo. I am thankful that I had that time so I can now help others on their own journeys.

My grandpa's fight with cancer will not end like mine. We know that the cancer will win this battle. But we also know that all will be well.

We will miss him terribly and I am very sad that he could not have lived longer..."

Within two short months, and after battling like a champion, my grandpa was gone. I, along with the rest of my family, was completely heartbroken. How could our Superman really be gone?

I felt a huge amount of anger surge within me. It was directed at the one and only thing that continued to rob me of precious things. I began to feel that no matter how hard I tried, I would never be free from cancer's suffocating grip.

With a heart that was still hurting and a tired body that was slowly healing, I tried to make the best of what was left of the summer of 2013. I spent time with my family and used the lazy days to try and bring some energy back to my downtrodden body and spirit. I also found myself looking forward to the end of the summer because there was an adventure waiting for me there. I was hoping that it would be something that would help me clear the cancer fog from my brain.

I had learned about an organization called First Descents. It is a non-profit organization that is committed to making a difference in the lives of young adult cancer survivors by treating them to a week of high adventure through one of three activities: kayaking, rock climbing, or surfing. I felt compelled to find out more about this amazing organization so I got on their website and before I knew it, I had signed up to be a part of one of their kayaking adventures.

I was excited for the opportunity, however, as the months passed by and the week of my adventure drew near, fear and anxiety overshadowed my excitement. I started to worry that maybe I had not healed enough from my last surgery. I certainly did not want to do any damage and have to go back to the surgery table to fix things. I was also worried because it seemed to be very bad timing. I would be gone for the whole first week of my kids' school year and would lose that precious alone time where I could get my preschool room ready.

A great debate waged in my mind. Do I go or do I not go? More than once, I found myself staring at a blank email that was addressed to the director of my kayaking adventure. I tried to find the right words to say that would explain why I would have to back out. Fortunately, I was never able to send that email. Something was telling me that I needed to go.

~HEARTACHE & HEALING~

On a beautiful August day, I sent my munchkins off to their first day of school, packed up my car, and headed off to Jackson, Wyoming, for a week-long kayaking adventure with First Descents. As I pulled up to the location that my GPS said was right, it looked deserted and I thought I had made a wrong turn somewhere. After a little scouting around, I finally found the correct building and timidly stepped into a room that was filled with complete strangers. I had a small, internal panic attack and wondered what I was getting myself into.

As the week progressed, any worry or fear that I had was slowly replaced with confidence, liberation, and joy. I had the assurance that I could continue on my journey because there were so many others who were in my same boat. Even though our cancer stories were very different, we all had the common thread of battling the beast and that meant that we would never be alone.

I also experienced empowerment over cancer. I realized that I did not have to let it dictate my thoughts and feelings any more. I had the power to put it in its place. Lastly, I experienced a colossal amount of pure happiness. Whatever muscles were not sore from the physical exertion of kayaking (and a few killer volleyball games) were sore from hours of deep belly laughter.

Before my First Descents adventure, if you would have told me that 12 complete strangers with very different personalities, opinions, and backgrounds, could come together for a week and forge an unbreakable bond, I would have laughed and said, "No way." How could such a bond be created in just a week?

There was only one word that could be used to describe what happened that week: magic. We were all meant to be there at that time, and I am so grateful that I followed through and listened to the prompting within myself that told me I should go.

It was extremely hard for all of us to say goodbye when our kayaking quest was over. We had come to the Snake River as strangers and we were leaving as family. We left with promises to stay in touch and to be there for each other no matter what. I could not have known then just how big of an impact this new family would make in my life as I drifted closer to the land of PTSD.

My aunt Cheri, my Superman Grandpa, and me at our "Fowlks Fighter" celebration
June 2013

On my First Descents adventure
August 2013

Forty-Four: THIS IS MY LIFE

*D*ay 763: *"Well now. You thought I was done with the daily cancer count, didn't you? So did I. I had closed the book. Moved on. A few days ago, a new book was cracked open. [A new journal started.] I am hoping to not get too far in this book.*

Let's back up a bit. For a few months now, I have been having some wrist pain. I thought it was just a side effect from the Arimidex medication that I am taking. [The pain] has been getting worse, so I talked to my oncologist about it. He did not think that it could be from the medication since I have been on it for a year. He suggested that I go to my regular doctor and have it checked out...

[I had my wrist checked] for carpal tunnel. The doctor did not think [that I was suffering from that.] I haven't had any numbness or tingling, just pain. She determined that I have a form of tendinitis. Then she continued with the rest of my exam. As she was checking the lymph nodes in my neck, she paused for just a little too long. She told me that the lymph nodes on my right side are swollen. She asked if I had any congestion or cold symptoms, which I do not. I started having a panic attack on the inside.

She ordered a neck CT, given my history and the fact that I am otherwise healthy. I told her that I would call my oncologist and see where he wanted me to have the CT scan done. She gave me a brace for one of my wrists and told me to try it out for a few weeks. I was basically just going through the motions at this point...I just wanted to get out of that office so I could call Dr. Chandramouli and get a scan scheduled.

As soon as my feet hit [the pavement], I was dialing the cancer center's number. I left [them] a message and then called Mark. I cried and felt the anxiety start to creep in. I could not believe that I had to go through this mind game again. Is it cancer? How bad is it? What am I going to have to do? Why do these things always happen so close to a weekend?

The cancer center called me back and I was able to schedule a CT scan for the following Wednesday. Great. Almost a whole week of the unknown. I was in complete turmoil on the inside. I had pretty much convinced myself that this was it. I was going to die. I went through the same roller coaster of emotions that I had gone through a little over two years ago.

I wanted to rip out my lymph nodes. I [also] wanted to rewind a few weeks to when I was feeling happy, healthy, and confident that everything was good. I fasted all day Monday and poured my heart out to my Father in Heaven. I begged and pleaded for my life. I went back and forth all day. 'It's going to be fine, it's not.'

As I was waiting for the kids to come home from school, I sat on the porch and started reading my scriptures. It was one of those 'I just opened the book and a scripture popped out' kind of moments. [I saw one] that I had already highlighted and it struck my heart.

Isaiah 58:8 'Then shall thy light break forth as the morning and thine health shall spring forth speedily: and they righteousness shall go before thee; the glory of the Lord shall be they rereward.'

It wasn't like a bolt of lightning or anything like that. I just had a good feeling that I was going to be okay.

I checked the footnotes and they led me to Jeremiah 30:17. 'For I will restore health unto thee, and I will heal thee of thy wounds, saith the Lord...' I feel like this was the answer to my prayers and fasting. It has been a challenge to hold on to these answers though. My thoughts are constantly toying with all of the 'What if's?' It has been so hard to keep a positive outlook.

I have to keep reminding myself that this is not a death sentence, even if it is cancer. I am not dead yet and I need to keep living and enjoying my life! This is why I fought so hard and why I will fight again if I need to..."

Day 764: "...I went into the cancer center on the 18th to have a neck CT. It was a very simple procedure. I was okay until I lied down on the table. Then I started shaking like I was cold. The nerves hit me all at once.

The scan literally took all of five minutes. Then I got to go home and wait some more. [The technician] told me that I should have the results the following day. Thursday came and I was a bundle of nerves. I taught preschool in the morning, but it was hard to concentrate. I kept expecting the phone to ring [and hear] the worst possible news. But it never rang. The preschool kids went home and as soon as I shut the door [behind them], I was calling the cancer center. I had to leave a message...

Finally about 4 pm, the phone rang and it was Dr. Chandramouli's number on the caller ID, but it wasn't him. Of course, he is out of town. But his PA, whom I have met before and really like, [was the one on the phone.]

He started off by questioning why the neck CT was ordered in the first place. I told him the story and he asked if I had a cold or anything like that. I haven't had one since June/July.

He said that those lymph nodes are definitely swollen, but the CT scan does not provide enough info to know why they are swollen. It's kind of a gray area as to what to do next. He gave me two choices, watch it for a while and see what it does or get a PET scan to see if there is measurable cancer there.

Umm--door #2 please. There is no 'let's wait and see' in my vocabulary at this point. I can't take any risks or chances. I am already living on a 2nd chance. [So we got a PET scan scheduled.]

My mind is convinced there is cancer there. Even though it really could be nothing. Mark and I both feel like there is going to be more than just nothing involved here though. I hope we are just gun-shy. I hope our gut feelings are wrong. We've been wrong before."

This is what my new life would look like? Happy, healthy times riddled with a few shots of anxiety bullets? I felt like I was on a train ride, hair blowing in the breeze, enjoying the beautiful scenery, when--WHAM! -- a switch is thrown and I am barreling out of control down an entirely different track, one with not so pretty scenery.

Day 766: "PET scan today. I am having a hard time really wrapping my head around this reality. Am I really worrying about the cancer growing again? After only two years?

As I was driving to the cancer center, I just felt really calm. Not a lot of nervousness, just anxious to get in, get the scan done, and go on with my day. I've spent so much time worrying about the outcome.

[But] I have not been given a death sentence. I am not dying today and I need to stop dwelling on that and just live my life!

[When it was time for the scan], the nurse took me back to a familiar place--the isolation recliner room. Then she injected the radioactive sugar into my IV. This little sugar attaches itself to any cancer spots that are one centimeter or larger. Then as I go through the scan, the cancer spots [if any] will light up. I have to wait an hour, in isolation, for the sugar to go through my body. I also have to drink a HUGE cup of liquid contrast. It's not terrible, but due to the fact that I had to drink it on an empty stomach, I was kind of gagging it down by the end.

It was very nice to have a whole hour of solitude...I was able to read in the Book of Mormon and ponder some things. I concluded that maybe I need to have more faith in God's plan for my family and me. It sounds weird as I write that because I do have a lot of faith--or I thought I did. But [in the past week and a half] I have let the fear over run the faith. I stopped trusting that God knows what is best for my family and me.

My family would survive without me. It would be hard, I know. It breaks my heart to think of their sorrow and the struggles that they would have. But they are strong and they could do it if they had to.

When [all of] this came up, I was pretty much convinced that I was going to die. Now, I am feeling that this is not a death sentence, at least not an immediate one. I am going to be around for a while; a long while is my hope.

After my hour [in isolation] was up, I changed into a gown and went into the PET scan room. I lay down on the table and [the technician] put my Piano Guys CD in so I could listen to music during the scan.

I had to lie there, on my back, with my arms up over my head, while the table moved back and forth through the scanner. It was actually very peaceful. I felt like I was in good hands. My grandpas were there with me, helping me to be strong.

In a half an hour, I was done. I changed my clothes and then drove home so I could wait for the results. I am hoping to hear tomorrow, but I am not counting on it.

I am so physically and emotionally drained right now. I've kind of slipped into 'numb' mode. [However,] I have definitely been lifted up more than once by love, prayers, and positive thoughts from everyone around me. I am so lucky to have so many amazing people in my life.

I had to fast for this scan, so I used it as an opportunity to fast and pray. My prayer is this--I just want a fighting chance. I need to have some hope that if it is cancer, I have a chance of beating it. I will do surgery, chemo, and radiation--whatever I have to do. I need to be here for my kids. I need to get them all through high school at least.

Please, dear Father. I will do <u>anything</u> if I can just raise my kids. Please let me raise my kids."

Forty-Five:

THE MOST THANKFUL
THURSDAY EVER

As I felt the recurring cancer nightmare swirling around me, I tried to maintain an "attitude of gratitude." Expressing gratitude had been key to battling the cancer before so I thought that it would be a good idea to start writing about some of the things that I was thankful for. I felt that maybe it would help take my mind off the present situation.

Since my blog had been a large part of my healing process, I decided to start a series of posts, which I titled my "Thankful Thursday" series. (Not original, I know, but how can you not pair "thankful" and "Thursday" together? It just makes sense.)

My "Thankful Thursday" posts became a wonderful way for me to reflect on my life and express gratitude for the incredible blessings that God had given me. As I wrote each post, I discovered that the hard times didn't seem so harsh and the good times felt a lot more delightful.

~ONE DAY AT A TIME~

The Thursday after my PET scan, I was keeping my fingers crossed that I would be able to have some great news to write about. I arose that morning after a restless night of tossing and turning. Although I had not slept well, my bed still provided a warm cocoon of comfort, so it was hard for me to drag myself out of it.

There was one thing that helped me rise and face the day. I knew that in just a few hours I would have the opportunity to spend time in one of the most beautiful places on earth; the temple. More than anything, I needed the renewal of the spirit that I knew I could feel by being in the temple.

Day 768: "I can't even describe to you the amount of relief I feel at this moment. This morning I was a basket case. I called the cancer center right at 9 A.M. and left a message to have someone call me with the PET scan results. Then I had to leave my phone in the car while we went into the beautiful Bountiful Temple.

I am so happy to have had the opportunity to spend time in the temple today. I was trying to let the spirit calm my troubled heart. I bawled [as I walked] past all the pictures of Christ. I [so desperately] wanted this nightmare to be over!

After we were done [in the temple], we rushed out to the car. I was in a dilemma. I wanted to check my phone, but I also didn't want to check my phone. I wanted to have a missed call, but I didn't want to have an 'I'm sorry, but we found cancer' message. There was no missed call.

So again, the anxiety and depression began to creep in. I was desperately trying to keep up a happy facade because it was such a beautiful occasion (we were attending a wedding), but I really just wanted to be home in my bed, curled up in a ball, trying not to think about dumb cancer.

[After the temple] we went to lunch with some of Mark's family. We were enjoying gigantic chunks of fresh cornbread when my phone started to vibrate in my lap. My oncologist's office [was] calling. This was it. The moment I have been waiting for and dreading for two weeks. I answered [the call] and stepped outside.

~THE MOST THANKFUL THURSDAY EVER~

It was Rick, the PA. My doctor is still out of town. [Rick] was happy to inform me that no cancer showed up on the PET scan. I could not believe it! I was so sure that he was going to be telling me that there was a tumor. The rest of the conversation is kind of a blur. I remember him saying that he would talk to Dr. Chandramouli when he gets back in town next week. He also said that we would have to watch a spot on my right lung, which is probably just scarring from radiation, [but still something that should be watched.] Then he thanked me because he said it was the best phone call he has made all week. I am sorry to all of the people he had to make bad phone calls to, but I am overjoyed that my phone call was a good one."

The power of one phone call continued to amaze me. With that simple call, I was immediately put back on the track with beautiful scenery. The detour track that we had to take had been a huge jolt of fear for all of us, especially my brave little munchkins. I know that any amount of anxiety that I had felt was small in comparison to what they had probably been feeling and that made my heart hurt.

From the very beginning of the journey, I had included them in the loop as much as possible. I made sure that they had ample time to ask questions, cry on shoulders, and be supported in whatever way they needed. Looking back, I wish that I wouldn't have let them know about the whole *"Is the cancer back?"* scare, at least not until I had definite answers. I did not realize, until after the fact, just how much anxiety it had created for them, particularly for my sweet Emma.

She happened to call me from school shortly after I found out the PET scan results. Ever the worrier, she was calling to make sure that it was okay for her teacher to put some hydrocortisone cream on her itchy bug bite. I told her that it was absolutely okay to do that but before she hung up I said, "Hey, Emma. Guess what?"

"What?" she replied.

"The doctor just called me and told me that there is no cancer. Isn't that awesome?" I said.

There was complete silence on her end followed by some sniffles. I could tell that her tender little heart was bursting. That, of course, was more than my mother's heart could take and I started crying as well.

"I love you, sweetheart," I choked out. "I will see you after school!"

That was the conversation, as I knew it. Later, her teacher told me what she had witnessed. She told me that during that phone conversation, Emma's countenance completely changed. After she hung up she crumbled, and Mrs. Benedum saw a look of instant relief spread across her face. It was as though she was finally able to release the fear that had consumed her and lay aside her brave face.

That afternoon as I sat down at the computer, I was overcome with gratitude as I typed the words, "*PET scan results are free and clear. No cancer was detected.*" As I hit the "publish post" button and pushed back from the desk, I let out a huge sigh of relief. I had dodged a bullet for now. Even though I knew that there would always be the possibility of having to dodge more, it felt so good to be safe for that moment in time.

Yes, it was unquestionably the most thankful Thursday ever but unfortunately, it only calmed the stormy waters for a moment. I was still drifting closer to PTSD land and one little Thankful Thursday was not enough to drop anchor.

Forty-Six:

THE CANCER HANGOVER

With the knowledge that smooth sailing doesn't last long on the stormy seas of life, I am still grateful that we are given some serene moments. Without them, we would not be able to have the strength to hang on for dear life when the swells rise and our ships are tossed about.

The days and weeks that followed my scare were pretty peaceful. I was still going through my "cancer hangover" (a term coined by my friend, Cyndi), but all things considered, I was doing okay.

Day 798: "Still the same old battle with the fatigue monster. I feel like I never get enough sleep, no matter how much sleep I get...I drag myself out of bed in the morning because I have to. I would love to stay in bed a lot longer. When I do get out of bed or try to stand up after sitting, I have to be careful because it takes a minute for my legs to work properly.

I am mostly good, but I am just not feeling like myself sometimes. That recurrence scare messed me up. I was going along really well. I had finally said goodbye to the cancer and was ready to forge ahead in my new life. But cancer will always be lurking in the shadows for the rest of my life.

It's like I am shackled to a ball and chain and have to drag it around with me. I hope and pray that as the years go by, I will be able to not have it be such a worry in my mind. Some days I am really able to feel peace about it. I do know that my life is in God's hands and whatever will be, will be. But it still doesn't take away the [human part of me who is ruled by fear.]"

Day 812: "My appointment with Dr. C went well. My blood looks good. He said that scans looked good as well. I also saw Dr. Leckman for my one year check-up. I can't believe it's been a year since I saw him. He said everything looks good as well.

Why can't I convince my silly brain that everything is okay then? I have had the Lord tell me through scriptures, and I have had two doctors tell me that everything is well. Why can't I really feel that?

I just keep waiting for the other shoe to drop. I am happy and living life, but I have that nagging fear that creeps around in the back of my brain.

Maybe it's because I was in a good place in my life when it all came crashing down. I was comfortable and happy and everything was really good. Maybe I am afraid to get comfortable again. I don't know. It's definitely still a bit of a roller coaster ride.

I love my life. I love my husband and kids and I truly am thankful to have the chance to stay here on earth a little while longer with them."

Day 880: "It has been almost two years since I finished chemo. I am amazed how this poison still affects my body. Chemo brain is real and some days it is really bad, others it is not. The best way to describe a bad day is that it is like walking through a fog all day long. It is like I have a cloud or cobwebs sitting on my head, and I just can't filter through them. My actions and responses feel sluggish. Multi-tasking is much harder than it used to be.

My body still has a lot of aches and pains. I have been pretty good about exercising daily. I can feel strength returning...

My mental health is still taking a huge hit. I'm sure it will for some time now. I still cannot convince myself that everything is gone. [I feel like the cancer] will just be sneaky and fester and grow. I am convinced that one day I will just be feeling great and then wham! I will get the 'you have cancer' phone call and our lives will be turned upside down again.

I try not to let my thoughts dwell here for too long. It's a dangerous place to be. I am just thankful that I am still able to go to the doctor every three months. I find a lot of comfort in that. But there is also a lot of anxiety that comes along with those visits. Every time one rolls around, the panic alarms in my head reset. 'What if something turns up this time?' It was sneaky before. It can be sneaky again."

Once again, I felt like I just could not escape cancer's grasp and my mental health was taking a huge hit. It seemed to be everywhere. When I looked at Facebook, I felt like all I saw was update after update about someone whose cancer had returned. It also seemed as though nearly every conversation I had concluded with, "Oh, by the way. Did you hear that (so and so's) cancer has come back?"

Part of the problem was also due to the reality that there were some really amazing people in my life who were still having the life squeezed out of them by cancer's ugly grip. Their struggles and the heartache I felt for them were a large part of why I had finally reached the shores of PTSD land.

Forty-Seven: MY FRIENDS

The death of my grandpa, my cancer recurrence scare, and the symptoms of my cancer hangover had brought me to the shores of PTSD land. Now, as I learned of the struggles that my friends were going through, my brain decided that it would like to take an extended vacation there.

One of my friends who was not doing well was Brian, a member of my FD (First Descents) family. Thanks to Facebook, email, and text messaging, our family could stay true to our promise of keeping in touch. It was so fun to continue our relationships and learn more about each other through social media stalking. (The friendly kind, not the creepy kind.)

Facebook also led us to know that by March of 2014, Brian was not doing well. Out of all the people in my FD family, he was the last one that I expected to die first. He was one of the most health conscious and positive people I have ever met. You couldn't help but be happy when you were around him. His smile and enthusiasm were infectious.

It had come as quite a shock to our entire group when we found out that his cancer had returned, and it was quickly ravaging his incredibly strong body. At the end of March his body could not take any more and he passed away, two weeks shy of his 27th birthday. It was a devastating loss for all who knew him.

Another friend, Tia, (who is also part of my FD family) was still forging ahead in her battle with Stage IV breast cancer. It was heartbreaking to read of all the setbacks and struggles of someone who was living with the disease day in and day out. I felt, and still feel, helpless. My moments of glory and triumph over cancer were stained with sadness as I thought of her, and so many others like her, who continue to live and fight with breast cancer.

It was also around that time that I was trying to help another friend, Carol, as she became a member of the "Cancer Club." Carol and I had a unique bond, although we had never really spent a lot of time together. I met her when I was PTA president. She was one of the volunteers who saved my bacon on more than one occasion.

I knew that Carol had been struggling with Crohn's disease for years, but now, her worst fears had come true. In January 2014, she was diagnosed with colon cancer that had metastasized to her liver. We were all heartbroken for her. Here was another young mother, her boys just 8 and 9 years old, who now had to face the challenging journey of fighting cancer and taking care of a family at the same time.

Her ride went up and down so many times over the months that followed. One moment we were so hopeful that she would make it through. The next, we were discouraged and wondering how she was ever going to make it.

I loved visiting with her, but it was incredibly hard to see the toll that cancer was taking on her body. I couldn't help but feel a huge amount of "survivor's guilt." Why was it that I could beat cancer and stay here with my kids while her body was slowly and painfully wasting away? I didn't love my kids any more than she loved hers. My kids didn't need me more than her kids needed her. How was it okay for me to stay and for her to go?

In thinking of all the tumultuous chaos that cancer was creating in my friends' lives, my brain started to shut down. I could no longer process rational thoughts about my own cancer. I started playing an intense mental game that I didn't think I would be able to win.

Day 951: "I am struggling. I feel unsettled. I feel as though something is off--not right. I haven't been experiencing huge amounts of pain, just some minor, but consistent, discomfort...I have [also] been feeling more fatigue. I try to brush it off because I've been pushing myself and exercising so much. Today while I was jogging, I felt tighter in my chest, a little more wheezy than usual.

Now, having said all of those things, I feel like a hypochondriac. Are these really things that need further investigation or am I just being jumpy because of Brian's death? I have been trying so hard to find some peace and comfort in all of this.

I really wish that [God could tell me] 'Don't worry. You're going to live a long, full life.' It's like as soon as I stop worrying about it, the little voice in the back of my head starts up saying, 'You have to worry. It's coming back. You are not going to live to see grandkids.'

I hate cancer and I hate the mind games that come along with it.

I asked Mark to give me a blessing tonight. Some of the things that stood out to me are:

-Through fasting and prayer, I will be able to receive personal revelation allowing me a glimpse of what my future holds.

-My caregivers will know what to do to help me.

-I will be able to have peace and comfort in knowing God's plan for me and my family.

-My family will be sensitive to my needs.

Now, when I think about these words and how I felt during the blessing, I feel as though my cancer journey is still going to continue. What I am trying to do now is to figure out how to be okay with that."

I spent the morning of the following day, Day 952, at the temple. I needed to shut out the screaming world and the constant barrage of thoughts of dying. I went with these questions churning in my heart: "*How can I ever be okay with dying while my kids are young?", "What can I do to not have the fear of cancer paralyze me?",* and *"What is the plan from here on out?"*

That day in the temple, I received different answers to those questions than I was expecting. I felt surrounded by loved ones who have passed on, and I knew that no matter what the future held for me, I would be able to thrive in any circumstance. I was, and continue to be, in the hands of a loving Father in Heaven who knows exactly what He is doing. I had (and continue to have) no need to be afraid.

> *Day 954: "I was hoping to go [to the temple] and receive the answer of 'Don't worry. The cancer is gone and won't return.' [But] that would be the easy answer. If that were the answer, I might start to forget things and be complacent. But if I always have cancer in the back of my mind, then I will always be able to more fully appreciate my life and everything in it.*
>
> *Unfortunately, along with that comes the problem of always thinking about the cancer. Sometimes my brain feels like it's going to explode. It is always so full of everything I keep shoving in there that goes along with all of my jobs. Then I start to feel like I am drowning. I feel like there is not enough time for me to prepare everything I would like to if it came time for me to go. This living thing is hard work."*

With Brian's death, the struggles of Tia and Carol, and my own physical and emotional state, I started to realize that although God was helping me as much as He could from His place in heaven, maybe I needed to talk to someone here on earth who could help me clear out the cobwebs and put things in their proper place. The only problem was, where could I go to find such a person?

Forty-Eight:

NO, YOU ARE NOT CRAZY

There is something about the actual diagnosis of a problem that gives you some sort of comfort. Even when that diagnosis is cancer, you feel like you at least have a jumping off point. You can begin to plan to either fix the situation, or prepare yourself for the inevitable. Either way, I feel that knowing what you are dealing with is always better than not knowing.

As I struggled to know what was happening to me and why I just couldn't push past the fear of the cancer coming back, I was happy that I found someone who led me to know that I was not crazy. I was, in fact, having a very normal reaction to some extremely traumatic experiences in my life.

Day 960: "I had a major meltdown on Sunday. I was feeling a little irritable all morning. Even at church, I was just not myself. By the time we got home, I felt like my insides were going to burst. I couldn't hold it in any longer. My brain literally ached from all the deep pondering I had been doing. I closed myself in my bathroom and just cried; sobbed is more like it.

~NO, YOU ARE NOT CRAZY~

*[When Mark got home], he could tell that something was wrong. He made
me his unofficial last appointment of the day and we had a little chat in our
room. He felt that I have been suffering from PTSD. I am pretty sure I
agree. We decided that it is probably a good idea that I meet with a
counselor. On Monday, I [scheduled] an appointment..."*

I met with a great counselor at LDS Family Services. She made me feel
comfortable and more importantly, she made me feel a lot less crazy. I knew that
I had made the right decision to meet with her and felt very blessed to have such a
smart husband/bishop who pointed me in the right direction.

During the session, we began by chatting about my family and about
different memories I had of growing up. We moved on to talking about my fears,
anxiety, anger, and everything else that was related to my cancer journey. The
counselor confirmed Mark's suspicions and told me that we were indeed dealing
with PTSD.

What does that entail? How does one overcome PTSD? One of the things
that she told me would be helpful was that I needed to find a way to reset my brain
when it went into panic mode. Whether it be through breathing exercises,
relaxation techniques, yoga, or listening to certain music, I needed to find the reset
that worked for my brain. That meant that I would need to start experimenting.

As I sat there listening to her suggestions, I kept telling myself, *"You
already know these things! Why haven't you thought about doing them?"* I had
been trying to teach my daughter, Abbie, to use some of those techniques to help
with her own anxiety issues, so why hadn't I thought to use them myself? I suppose
sometimes it just takes someone looking in from the outside to help bring to our
attention the things that we already know.

My counselor also made a great connection that I had not thought of
before; how my birth order affects my personality and the way that I was
processing (or not processing) things. Since I am the oldest in my family, I have
always had a kind of caretaker/leader personality. Because of that mentality, it
was hard for me to entertain the thought of dying and leaving my family.

I constantly asked myself questions like: Who would take care of everything that needed to be taken care of? Who would cart the kids around to their various activities? Who would make sure the dog was fed and the dishes were done? The leader/caregiver part of me just could not understand how all those items would get done if I weren't here. Even though the rational side of my brain knew that ultimately my family would survive, they would figure things out and life would move on for them, the irrational side just could not see how it would work. I think there is another term for that...it's called "control freak."

The more I talked and opened up to my counselor, the lighter I felt. The load that had been pressing down upon my tired shoulders had shifted slightly. I became more aware of what I needed to be doing to make sure that I was in a good place and stayed there. I also had the realization that *I* had the power to overcome the feeling that the rug was going to be pulled out from under me. *I* had the power to tell cancer to stay in the back corner of my brain and not taunt me anymore.

On the way home, I had a very enlightening and spiritual moment of clarity. As I was digesting everything my counselor and I had discussed, I had the very strong impression that God loved me. Of course, this was something that I already knew, but for a very brief moment, I felt encompassed in unseen arms. I felt as though my heart was going to burst and there are no words to describe the intense feeling of love that filled the van as I drove home.

God knew that I wasn't crazy. He knew that what I had been dealing with emotionally was extremely real and very difficult and He wanted me to know, without any doubt, that I was His daughter, and that He loved me.

"It's going to take some time and I am going to have to make a very conscious effort to reset my brain when it gets anxious. But, like I tell my kids all the time, we can do hard things."

Forty-Nine: CARRYING ON

As time rolled along and I began experimenting with ways to reset my brain, I started to make some progress. It was slow progress, but I was moving in the right direction and that was good.

I was gaining some ground over the fear and starting to really show the cancer who was the boss. Then the real test came when I was faced with saying goodbye to my friend, Carol. How would I react to that? Would I still be able to stay on top of my fears?

Day 1,018: "I lost another friend today to this horrible thing we call cancer. My friend, Carol, passed away this morning after a short battle with Stage IV colon cancer...it is a blessing that she is free from pain, but so sad for her two little boys and husband.

Surprisingly, I am doing well. I was worried that as she kept taking a turn for the worse, my PTSD would kick in and I would have another panic attack. [So far, I have been able to keep that in check, but I have been] suffering a lot from 'survivor's guilt.' I feel horrible that her boys now have to grow up without her in their daily lives...

~ONE DAY AT A TIME~

Carol is my hero. I love her and I really wish that it could have been a different outcome for her."

The last moments that I spent with Carol, on this earth, will always linger in my mind and on my heart. As I walked into her room, I could not believe my eyes. She was so small and frail. My heart broke into about a million pieces as I realized that this would be my last conversation with her until we meet again in heaven.

In her limited state of consciousness, she gave me a weak, half of a smile; her signature smile, the one that I loved so much. I miss that smile. I held her hand and the only words that I could find were, "I'm sorry. I'm so sorry, Carol." I knew that we both wanted a different outcome.

We chatted for a few minutes, or rather, I rambled on and on while Carol struggled to stay awake. Then the time came to say goodbye. It was so hard to leave that room, knowing that it would be the last time I would be with her. I gave her as much of a hug as I could. She felt and looked so breakable in that moment. I also told her that I loved her. I gave her beautifully manicured hand another squeeze and Mark and I made our way back to our car.

I lost it as soon as I sank down onto the seat. The pain was almost more than I could endure. I tried to force the image of her delicate body out of my mind, but I just couldn't. Through my tears, I told Mark, "This cancer cannot come back. I don't want to die that way."

That night I went to bed with thoughts of Carol, Brian, and my grandpa swimming around in my brain. Three people that I loved and cherished so much were gone, having moved onto paradise. I knew that I would see all of them again and that they were free from pain and sorrow. I also knew that they would always linger in my heart, but that didn't take the pain away and I cried myself to sleep anyway.

I attended a funeral once where one of the speakers said something that pricked my heartstrings. I can't remember the exact quote, but basically, she said that when someone dies, we are sad because of love. When we love someone so much, it seems unbearable when they depart from this life and enter the next.

Then she said, "I would much rather endure the sadness for a while than to not have love in my life."

I agree with that statement 100%. I am grateful for all the love that I have in my life. It was love that carried me through the darkest stages of my journey. It was love that gave me the courage to take another step forward and it is love that keeps me going.

As I finish writing this book, it has been a little over four years since my diagnosis. The storm of my cancer has been stilled for a moment and I am relishing in the opportunity to catch my breath. Each day I feel a little stronger and little wiser.

I have changed my thought process from "if" it comes back to "when" it comes back. For some reason, just switching that one little word has made all the difference for me. Maybe it will come back and maybe it won't. In the meantime, I am healthy and I am alive. My goal is to not just survive for the rest of my life, but to thrive. Some days, I am really good at that. Others, I am not. The hard part is to make sure that I am not beating myself up too much on the days that I don't thrive. I just have to pick myself up, dust myself off, and start over the next day.

At the beginning of this book, I mentioned three goals that I had set to keep me focused on what I aim to accomplish in writing this memoir:

Goal #1: To inspire people who are in the trenches of a war with cancer.

I hope that if you are one that has had that life changing phone call, you have been able to find some comfort in these pages. I take my job as a cancer survivor very seriously and I know that part of that job is to help others through their nightmares.

223

To those who are in the midst of the battle, I say, "Keep going." Keep putting one foot in front of the other. It will be very hard and at times you will feel as though there is no end in sight, <u>but you have to keep going</u>. Enjoy the good days and allow yourself to be a slug on the couch on the bad days.

Use this time to take care of you, inside and out. *Let people help you.* Ask God what His plan is for you and then, look around you. I can say with certainty that there is someone who is worse off than you are. Reach out a hand to help them and you will be amazed at how much better you can and will feel.

And to my survivor sisters and brothers who may be reaching the end of their mortal journey, my prayers are with you. I won't pretend to know how it feels to be where you are. With all the thoughts of death that swirled around me, I never reached that point of <u>knowing</u> that the cancer would take me.

As I have been honored to know women and men who have found themselves in this situation, my thoughts about survivorship have taken on a different shape. The elation that I feel as I reflect on how I was able to move past cancer is always darkened by the deep sadness I feel as I think about those who will have a different outcome. My friends, you are the true heroes of this disease and I love you.

Goal #2: To inspire mothers.

I hope that from the words on these pages you get the sense that my job as a mother is the most important thing that I do every single day. I begged and pleaded to be able to stay here and raise my kiddos. For reasons only God knows, I am still here. I try to live each day being the best mommy that I can be. I don't want to take a single moment for granted.

Some days I feel like I could win the "Mother of the Year" award: everyone seems happy, the house is marginally clean, and I have only raised my voice once or twice in the process. Other days, the raging lunatic mom finds her way to the surface and I have to take a lot of deep breaths and forgive myself for whatever the raging lunatic has done. This is how it will be as long as I am a mom, and that's okay. There is no such thing as a perfect mom, just perfect moments.

Because I love my job as a mother so much, I can't help but be sad when I hear of other young mothers who have had to leave this life and move on to the next. Sometimes it is unbearable to think of the children they have to leave behind for a time. When I do hear of these situations, I immediately begin to pray for those families that will now have to learn to live each day without their mommy. I also hug my own kids a little tighter and whisper a silent prayer of gratitude. Then I ask, "What do you need me to do, Father? You kept me here for a reason. Please help me to know where you need me to be and who you need me to help."

As I turn to God, my heart is comforted and I am reminded that there is a great plan of happiness for everyone. Sometimes it is hard for us to see how mothers leaving their young children could be part of a plan of happiness, but we have to remember that God sees what we can't see. We have to exercise faith and trust in His plan. We can't know the answers to all the "Why's", but we can make the most of the time that we have by seeking to know what God would have us do with the time that we have been blessed with.

Goal #3: To share my love and testimony of our Savior, Jesus Christ.

Finally, I leave you with my thoughts about the one person who helped me more than anyone else--my Savior, Jesus Christ. He lifted me when I couldn't stand on my own two feet. He sent earthly and heavenly angels to help me in my darkest hours. He brought peace to my troubled heart and helped me realize that life is such a precious gift. It's something that we cannot take for granted and it is also something that we should be enjoying, not just enduring.

The Savior of the world loves us so much and He wants to help us. You will always have a best friend when you allow Him to be a part of your life. Once you let Him in, you will never be the same. He will be there to help you through the good times and the bad, one day at a time.

EPILOGUE

Four years. It has now been a little over four years since my diagnosis. I have come a long way in those four years; yet at times, I feel like I am right back in those beginning stages, battling fear and anxiety. The PTSD kicks in and I go through a slight mental breakdown. Usually this happens right around the time of my follow-up appointments with my oncologist. I start noticing every little thing that doesn't feel "normal" and make note of it so I can talk to him about it. Then I do the whole "you're crazy/no you're not" talk in my head and try to convince myself that I am just being silly.

Yes, the mental game is still exhausting. I would say that 80% of the time, I don't think about it. Eighty percent of the time, I am living life to the fullest, enjoying my second chance, and thriving in my circumstances.

But the remaining 20% of the time is spent trying to convince myself that I am healthy; that the new ache in my back is just a tweaked muscle, my IBS flare up is just an IBS flare up, my increased fatigue is just because I need more sleep, and so on. Every time I leave a doctor's office with a clean bill of health, I feel grateful, but I also feel a bit of trepidation. It's almost as though my anxious brain will not rest until one of these doctors tell me, "I'm sorry. The cancer is back." Man! I really, really, really, despise what cancer has done to me mentally!

I can take the physical changes...

*The scars- I love them. Every time I see them, they remind me that I did a really hard thing and I was given a second chance.

*The lack of estrogen- I will say that I mostly love this. I really love not having to deal with "that time of the month" physically, although mentally, I feel like I still go through phantom PMS and get a bit cranky, which is weird. One thing that I have not loved about the lack of estrogen is the development of "melasma" or a darkening of my upper lip due to the hormone change in my body. In other words, I have a hairless mustache that won't go away. Sure, I am probably the only one who notices it, but it still bugs me. I'll get over it though.

But the mental changes? They are a challenge sometimes. *SIGH* Cancer is blah. BUT! I... am... alive...and it's so good to be alive! I will take the mental anguish, the weird pains that are probably just weird pains; I will even take the mustache, because I have a great life.

I know that there is a God who loves me and knows me. I know that whatever the next step is for me, I will be able to do it because I have His help and guidance. I know that I am here for a reason and every single day I pray to know where God needs me, what He needs me to do, and who He needs me to help. I also have a pretty amazing network of family and friends who fill my life with joy and continue to love and support me through all of life's crazy adventures.

Four years. Four years of taking life one day at a time. Four years of living, loving, and growing. Yes, today is definitely a happy day. A day of celebration, and let's be honest, will probably include some chocolate in one form or another. Life is good and I am so happy to be living it.

(Taken from the blog post "8-19-15" on www.desiraeogden.com)

August 2015

Pictures taken by Holly Robinson Photography- 2012

Breast Cancer Resources

www.breastcancer.org: *This was my go-to place to learn more about all the medical jargon that I did not understand. Obviously, your doctor is your best resource to clarify anything you don't understand, but this is a good place to go on the nights when you can't sleep and feel like you need to educate yourself.*

www.youngsurvival.org: *This is a great resource for women who are diagnosed at a young age, but the information is useful for anyone who has been diagnosed with breast cancer, regardless of age.*

www.facebook.com/groups/yssutah/: *This is the support group that I belong to. It was helpful for me to have a resource such as this so that I could connect with other young breast cancer* *patients. I encourage you to seek out similar groups in your own area. If you cannot find a group in your area, please connect with this group or go to www.youngsurvival.org and let them assist you in finding a support group.*

www.metavivor.org: *This is a wonderful organization that donates money and other resources to funding research for women and men who are living with Stage IV (Metastatic) Breast Cancer. If you are looking to donate money to a good cause, this is your good cause.*

www.imagerebornfoundation.org: *This is a foundation that provides weekend and one-day retreats for breast cancer survivors. Such a phenomenal experience. I highly recommend it. They even have travel scholarships if you need assistance in getting to the locations.*

www.firstdescents.org: *I could not give you a resource list without including this organization on it. It was a game changer for me. First Descents is available to any cancer survivor from the ages 18-39. Their weeklong adventures will help you heal in so many ways. They also have a program for cancer patients age 40-49.*

About the Author

Desirae Ogden is a mother to four beautiful, strong, and super cool kids. When she is not carting those kids to and from activities, she enjoys blogging, playing the piano, feeding her crafting disease, and doing what she can to help others.

As a survivor of cancer herself, her mission is to spread hope and love to those who are struggling not only with cancer, but also with the variety of other trials life brings. Her greatest desire is to love others through their journeys as she was loved through hers.

Desirae and her husband, Mark, live in Murray, Utah with their 4 children.

Desirae blogs at
www.desiraeogden.com

Made in the USA
Las Vegas, NV
08 December 2020